Coffee Shop Conversations

Coffee Shop Conversations

Evangelical Perspectives on Current Issues

Edited by

Russell L. Meek and
N. Blake Hearson

WIPF & STOCK · Eugene, Oregon

COFFEE SHOP CONVERSATIONS
Evangelical Perspectives on Current Issues

Wipf & Stock
An Imprint of Wipf and Stock Publishers
199 W. 8th Ave., Suite 3
Eugene, OR 97401
www.wipfandstock.com

ISBN 13: 978-1-61097-967-2
Manufactured in the U.S.A.

Contents

Contributors

Russell L. Meek, Adjunct Instructor and doctoral student, Midwestern Baptist Theological Seminary. He is associate editor of *Journal for the Evangelical Study of the Old Testament* and an assistant book review editor for *Journal of Hebrew Scriptures*.

N. Blake Hearson, Associate Professor of Old Testament and Hebrew, Midwestern Baptist Theological Seminary. He earned his Ph.D. and M.Phil. degrees in Hebraic and Cognate Studies from Hebrew Union College. He also holds an M.Div. degree from Gordon-Conwell Theological Seminary, and MA and BA degrees from Wheaton College.

Matthew Arbo, Assistant Professor of Ethics, Midwestern Baptist Theological Seminary. He earned a Ph.D. and M.Th. from Edinburgh University.

William K. Bechtold III, Adjunct Instructor, Midwestern Baptist Theological Seminary and Program Coordinator of Religion, Park University. He holds an M.Div. from Midwestern Baptist Theological Seminary.

Walter Kaiser, Jr., President Emeritus at Gordon-Conwell Theological Seminary. He earned a Ph.D. from Brandeis University.

Thor Madsen, Professor of New Testament, Ethics, and Philosophy and Dean of the College, Midwestern Baptist Theological Seminary. He earned a Ph.D. from the University of Aberdeen.

William R. Osborne, Assistant Professor of Biblical and Theological Studies at College of the Ozarks. He previously served as a missionary and faculty member at the Cameroon Baptist Theological Seminary. He is the managing editor of *Journal for the Evangelical Study of the Old Testament*.

Matthew Soerens, US Training Specialist, World Relief. He earned a Bachelor's Degree from Wheaton College and a Master's Degree from DePaul University's School of Public Service.

Corwin Smidt, Professor of Political Science Emeritus and Research Fellow for the Henry Institute for the Study of Christianity and Politics, Calvin College. He earned a BA in political science and history from Northwestern University and an MA and Ph.D. from the University of Iowa in political science.

Foreword

SO MUCH OF THE Bible, and thus so much of the Bible's theology, takes place around conversations. Three unknown visitors show up one day at the tent of Abraham. Sarah makes tea and listens in on the talk around the table and hears about a child of promise to be born in her old age. Or a decorated military officer in the army of Syria, a man called Naaman, hears about a conversation between a prison girl from Israel and his wife. Mrs. Naaman relays the conversation that leads to her husband's miraculous healing from leprosy.

A discussion is a conversation with an agenda. The psalms are filled with this kind of stuff. "O God, why do you cast us off forever?" "Has the Lord's steadfast love ceased forever?" "Has God forgotten to be gracious?" "Has he in anger shut up his compassion?" "O God, do not keep silent, do not hold your peace or be still, O God!" Conversations flow into the New Testament as well. Paul describes his conversion to King Agrippa in a conversation. Jesus has an all-night conversation with Rabbi Nicodemus. We do not know what Jesus and Zacchaeus talked about at the dinner they shared after the sycamore tree encounter, but whatever it was, it led to repentance and a different kind of life for the little man everybody had hated before.

Conversations can be deep or shallow, casual or serious, but they invariably take place as an encounter between an "I" and a "thou." They happen at a level of verbal engagement when we have moved beyond the formal courtesies of cordiality—Good morning! Have a nice day! How's the weather looking?—and have reached the point of listening and responding to another person. One-way monologues are not conversations. They are soliloquies. I once had a conversation with a person about a job I was being offered. He talked nonstop about himself, the institution he ran, the ideas he thought I would be interested in, talk, talk, talk . . . but no listening, no dialogue, no conversation. I took another job. Having a conversation means that we have to shut up long enough to hear what someone else is saying. Real conversations are born out of mutual humility.

Such conversations can lead to faith. Jesus once had a conversation with a disreputable woman at Jacob's Well. Jesus did not begin that conversation by telling the woman of Samaria everything he knew about her past or by reminding her of the law of God or even by revealing his real identity as the Messiah. Jesus began with a simple question: "May I have a drink of water?" From that simple sip of home-poured H2O would flow "streams of living water": living water that brought transformation to this friendless woman and a great revival to her hometown.

Jacob's Well, where Jesus and this woman shared a simple drink of water, still stands today. I have been there. Today it is more of a tourist trap than a genuine place to meet and talk, but it is not hard to imagine what a garrulous watering hole it would have been in Jesus's day. Jacob's Well was what Floyd's barber shop was for the men of Mayberry on *The Andy Griffith Show* and what the Boston bar in *Cheers* was for a later generation of twenty-somethings. This is what the coffee shop has become for our generation today. Coffee shop culture began in the cafés of Rome and the salons of Paris. From there it spread to England, North America, and indeed all around the world. I just returned from a visit to Jakarta, Indonesia, which now boasts of more than twenty-five Starbucks! I love to go to coffee shops and just listen to the edges of conversations. You hear people talking about all kinds of things: politics, sports, broken hearts, missed opportunities, new romances, what's happening at work, issues of the day, and God. In fact, God is often just beneath the surface in conversations about the issues of the day and all the other stuff that comes out over a cup of java.

This book allows us to listen to thoughtful conversations about some of the pressing moral and spiritual questions of our day. Should the coffee we drink be fair trade or not? What should a Christian think about immigration policy and about immigrants themselves? The economy is on everyone's mind, but why should Christians care about the Dow Jones Industrial Average? Is making a budget a spiritual discipline? In a sex-saturated culture, how should Christian couples think about birth control? Or universal healthcare? Or military service? Or politics itself?

There is more to be said, of course, about each of these issues than the authors of these essays can present in the short compass of this volume. But each of these essays is a great conversation starter. Because Jesus Christ is the Lord of life—of all life—none of these issues can be dodged or swept under the rug. Jesus told his disciples to go into the world and make disciples among all the nations. That means we have a covenant of dialogue with all persons everywhere, none of whom is beyond the reach of God's redeeming grace. These coffee shop conversations can be a springboard to faith.

Timothy George
Dean of Beeson Divinity School of Samford University
General editor of the *Reformation Commentary on Scripture.*

Preface

THE COMPILATION OF ESSAYS in this book grew out of experiences that Russell had some time ago. As a college student, he spent many hours at a coffee shop near his campus, discussing current events and political issues. At the time, he did not know how to reconcile the various opinions he heard with his newfound faith in Christ. While there were any number of books devoted to singular topics such as just war and Christian involvement in politics, there was no single book that introduced the responses of seasoned conservative Christians to multiple thorny issues. Now, some years later, Russell and Blake feel a call to bring both academic research and a mature Christian perspective to help young believers in similar situations.

The editors believe that, as Christian scholars and churchmen, they are called to aid in the education and discipleship of God's church. It is not enough for Christian scholars to research and write only for each other, becoming lost in minute details and losing sight of the needs and concerns of the body of Christ. They therefore decided to create a volume that addresses current issues that often come up among friends over coffee—"coffee shop conversations," as it were. To that end, they recruited the contributors to this volume because they share the same passion for academic research that seeks to help in the growth of the church. It is their hope that this volume will enable Christians—especially those in a collegiate setting—to engage the culture around them through biblically informed conversations.

Each of the essays in this volume addresses a particular issue that is relevant to the Western church. It has not been the authors' aim to reflect every stance that could be taken on an issue, but instead they seek to offer readers a way to think about each issue from a Christian perspective, that is, in a way that is governed by the biblical text and faith in Jesus Christ. Naturally, even among admittedly conservative Christians, there are many opinions on the topics in this book. As such, the book is not intended to solve a given problem definitively but rather to introduce the topic from a reasoned stance that takes faith and the Bible seriously. Hopefully readers of this volume will be better equipped to engage the world in which they live and glorify God by their thoughts and actions.

The editors sincerely thank the contributors of this volume for giving their time and expertise. Their work demonstrates accessible scholarship and a perspective that integrates faith and life. This volume would not have been possible without them. They would also like to thank Wipf and Stock for their commitment to this project, especially Christian Amondson, whose patience and guidance has been invaluable.

Russell would like to thank his wife, Brittany Meek. She has repeatedly demonstrated that "he who finds a wife finds a good thing, and has obtained favor from Yahweh" (Prov 18:22). He would also like to thank Blake Hearson and Neal Nelson, whose discipleship and friendship have been more meaningful than they can know.

Blake would like to thank his wife Jennifer for all of her encouragement, his daughters Emma and Claire for helping him see life through the eyes of a child, and Midwestern Baptist Theological Seminary for granting him a sabbatical in which to finish this project. He would also like to give special acknowledgment to Russell Meek as the book you have before you was originally formulated in his mind through his love for God and the church.

Introduction

THIS BOOK IS A compilation of essays written by evangelical scholars who are seeking to provide Christians with a biblical perspective on various issues relevant to the twenty-first-century church. Each essay tackles a particular issue and gives an evangelical response that both calls Christians to engage the wider culture and provides a possible avenue in which to do this. It is our hope that the essays will open the door for wider cultural involvement and provide readers with a biblical model for addressing issues that face our culture today.

N. Blake Hearson examines the idea of Sabbath rest and whether or not the Sabbath still applies to contemporary Christians. Most Christians agree that the Ten Commandments are still binding, but do not know what to do with the fourth commandment. Hearson argues that it still applies in principle and is of great benefit to our well-being.

Russell L. Meek and William K. Bechtold look at the issue of Fair Trade, arguing that a biblical view of the poor demands that Christians today engage in fair trading practices.

Matthew Soerens writes a stirring essay on the plight of immigrants in the United States today. He argues from Scripture that believers must love the foreigner and he offers a way forward for immigration policy that respects both the law and the dignity of the foreigner.

William R. Osborne examines the "Quiverfull" movement within evangelicalism, concluding that Christians are not prohibited from managing the size of their families, but that they must take care regarding the type of birth control used in order to protect human life.

Walter C. Kaiser, Jr. looks at the recent economic recession. He notes the proper biblical response of Christians to money and follows this by analyzing the causes that have led to the current economic woes. Finally, he points to several options for long term financial stability such as a flat tax rate and the dangers of other philosophies such as the dispersion of money from the wealthy to the poor.

Matthew Arbo examines the debate over health care in light of the recent United States Supreme Court decision regarding universal health care. He argues ultimately that the evangelical response to health care must strive always to bear witness to the Healer.

Corwin Smidt writes about the divisive political climate in the United States today. He argues that Christians must refuse to judge the faith of others based on political affiliation. Furthermore, as Christians try to engage in politics for the glory of God, we must be willing to sacrifice the good for the sake of the perfect, or end up with neither.

Thor Madsen addresses the issue of warfare and Christian discipleship, arguing that the pacifist position is untenable and that Christians can justifiably engage in war.

Over Worked and Stressed Out

What Can the Sabbath Teach Us about Truly Living?

N. Blake Hearson

Introduction

WE LIVE IN A busy society. That fact is no surprise to anyone. Technology, while helpful, has filled our lives with more tasks. We can now work while driving and text or talk during lunch. There are no times that are off limits for accomplishing the tasks we feel we must do. This has, in turn, created the perceived need to do more in less time. As a result, technology gives us more leisure time which we fill with other tasks, increasing the demands and pressure on our lives. We feel the anxiety of trying to get everything done and outperform everyone else. Having a relaxed life has become so unusual that there are more and more news stories about people simplifying their lives or getting away from the demands of technology and life in American society.

Modern churches take full advantage of multimedia and busy schedules, doing their best to maximize volunteers and compete for time in the lives of their parishioners. It is often these very same churches that present whole series on balancing life and work and making sure that people carve out daily time with God. It was not always this way in our culture. It was not that many years ago that many parts of the United States enforced "blue laws" that required a day off on Sunday. Some of these laws required businesses to be closed all day on Sunday. Eventually these laws were eroded so that businesses were only closed on Sunday morning and modified so that no alcohol could be sold during that time. Of course, this restriction disappeared with time and now there is only a slight vestige of uniqueness remaining to Sundays in the vast majority of the United States.

This change has not been without effect on the Christian culture. The restaurant chain Chick-fil-a has made the conscious decision to close on Sundays so that its work force can go to church and have a break. Yet, the fact that the Chick-fil-a policy is so widely known and commented on shows just how out of character it is for our society. Many conservative Christians honor this stance with a somber nod and the feeling that it is the right decision. However, honoring the policy in principle does not stop them from going to a different restaurant after church with friends.

Our rapidly changing and accelerating culture and its effect on Christians should give us pause, but, ironically enough, it does not. Most Christians feel that some sort of rest on Sunday is a good idea, but they do not feel bound to any particularities. Many Christians view Sunday as a Sabbath of sorts, which for them constitutes a break from work, time for a nap, and maybe watching sports on television. Indeed, most modern American Christians view the Sabbath as an antiquated law from the Old Testament that has no bearing on them in the here and now. Yet, the Sabbath functions as an anchor point for the entire story of creation and the identity of Israel. Moving forward through Scripture, the command to observe the Sabbath occupies a pivotal point in the Ten Commandments, and the prophets and the New Testament have significant teachings on the Sabbath as well. Given the major role the Sabbath plays in the Bible, it is shocking that the Sabbath command is the only one of the Ten Commandments that Christians seem to ignore. At the same time, the rapidity of life has brought us to a place of turmoil and exhaustion. We need to look closely at the idea of Sabbath in Scripture and see that its principles offer a way to find peace and rest.

In many ways our culture has come to view the idea of Sabbath—in terms of stopping activity—as a burden. Noted theologian Marguerite Shuster states, "To rest from our labors because the world has already been created, and our final trust rests in God and not in ourselves, goes flatly against the violent manipulativeness and rabid self-reliance that permeate our whole culture, not to mention the relentless acquisitiveness that seems to head the list of our values."[1] However, this negative cultural attitude may

1. Shuster, "Response," 83.

have been true for early Jewish communities as well. Jesus admonished the Pharisees about the constant emphasis they placed on *doing* the commandments of Torah perfectly which made keeping both Sabbath and the other laws irksome and discouraging.[2] The focus of the Jewish teachers and early community had come to be on their own power and control to do everything right. The later rabbinical teachings seek to correct this negative attitude by emphasizing that the Sabbath should be welcomed with joy.[3]

Among both Jewish and Christian communities, past and present, the negative attitude toward keeping the Sabbath is grounded in a lack of understanding of its nature and purpose. The classic perception of the Sabbath is that it is a time when one does not have to work, but one cannot do anything fun either. The aforementioned blue laws and obligatory church or synagogue service attendance no doubt contributed to this perception.[4] Biblical and theological scholar Dennis T. Olson notes that, "The Old Testament Sabbath may be one of the most strongly countercultural concepts in the Bible in relation to our modern society and its values."[5] Ultimately, Sabbath becomes a different form of work in the view of the all-important "I" of our society. Rest is an obligation rather than something we want to do. This distorted picture of the Sabbath comes from both a fundamental misunderstanding about what the Sabbath is and an assumption of discontinuity between the Old and New Testaments.

Genesis and the Sabbath

In order to understand the Sabbath and where it should lead us, a brief overview of the biblical ideas about Sabbath is in order. Naturally, we start at the beginning—the end of the acts of creation in Gen 2:1–3 (NASB). The passage reads, "Thus the heavens and the earth were completed, and all their hosts. By the seventh day God completed His work which He had done, and He rested on the seventh day from all His work which He had

---

2. Matt 23:4.

3. As a husband welcomes his bride. Genesis Rabbah 11:8 on Gen 2:3.

4. It is beyond the scope of this essay to explore the transition from Saturday to Sunday as the point of Sabbath observance in the church or whether Sunday really serves as a replacement for the Sabbath in the Christian tradition. There are many resources available for those interested in learning more about this transition. See Olson, "Sacred Time" 23–25 as a starting point.

5. Olson, "Sacred Time," 30.

done. Then God blessed the seventh day and sanctified it, because in it He rested from all His work which God had created and made." In this passage we find that the Sabbath is actually the very last thing that God creates. Everything else is finished and complete, but creation as a whole is not complete until the Sabbath is put in place. God then goes on to bless the Sabbath, an act that is usually reserved for animate beings. The creation of human beings is usually understood to be the ultimate creation, the crowning act of creation to which all other created things lead. Yet, mankind's creation is not the final act. Sabbath rest is. In a very real sense, Sabbath, and not mankind, unifies and brings all of creation together.

God blesses the seventh day and calls it holy specifically because He rests on it. Sabbath has this unifying effect because God rests on that day. Why does God rest? The God of monotheism does not need to rest. God does not grow tired or weary.[6] Expenditure of energy does not deplete God in some way. Therefore, the idea of God resting on the Sabbath must have something else behind it.

While it is only implied, the idea of rest is associated with completion. At this point in the narrative, all is created so that there is nothing lacking. We have seen throughout the creation story that each successive thing created is, in some way, incomplete. Darkness and light have to be set apart. Water and land must have boundaries set between them. Plants need light and moisture. Animals need plants. Humanity needs the entire ecosystem and is responsible for continuing to maintain it and keep it in order. Indeed, any who study the creation story see a certain parallel and pairing between the first six days.[7] One rabbinic story notes this pairing as well as the fact that the seventh day, the Sabbath day, is left without a partner.[8] The final day is both incomplete and yet is the completion of creation. It looks back on creation and God rests in it. At the point of Sabbath, all that is needed is present. Nothing is lacking. Perfection has been achieved.

The fact that God rests on the Sabbath also means that creation has a purpose beyond function and action. Creation is complete so that fellowship with God is possible. The Sabbath is the period in which the fellowship takes place. Fellowship in this instance means trusting and resting in God based on His perfect provision via creation. Men and women will continue to work in creation and in this way reflect the creative nature of God, but

6. Isa 40:28.
7. See Matthews, *Genesis 1–11:26*, 115–6.
8. Genesis Rabbah 11:8.

the work is not the goal; trust and fellowship with God is. They will not forget the purpose of creation because they will rest in God's provision and not their own accomplishments. They will trust God because he rested, thereby proving the trustworthiness of what he had made. There is no more certain statement that God has provided all that is needed and that he can be trusted than the idea that he is able to cease and to rest. Fellowship with God is possible because there is no need or lack that can keep people from it. Adam and Eve do not need to *do* anything to have fellowship with God and rest in his presence.

The Sabbath's role in the creation narrative is to show that it is incumbent upon all creation to trust God. If the nature of creation is such that God illustrates that it is complete through rest, how much the more should human beings trust in God? The Sabbath looks back on creation and says it is complete, but as with Jesus's words on the cross, the story does not end there. The Sabbath also looks forward to fellowship with God and his creation. The completion provides for the fellowship—the rest that comes from trusting in God's provision.

Enter the fall. With the failure of humanity, creation and all that was in it became twisted and tainted, but God remained the same. Creation was no longer complete, so Sabbath rest took on a more redemptive role. The certainty of all needs being met in the world was lost with the sin and rebellion of humanity, but trusting in God to meet all of one's needs remained. As God worked toward the redemption of humanity through Israel, the Sabbath became a command to realize that redemption in a practical way: trust in God to provide and rest in the assurance of that provision.

Exodus and the Sabbath

This idea of the redemption and restoration of the relationship between humanity and God on the Sabbath is most readily apparent in the narrative about God's provision of the manna for the people in the wilderness and how that provision changed on the Sabbath day. The relevant part of the story occurs in Exod 16:21–30 (NASB):

> They gathered it morning by morning, every man as much as he should eat; but when the sun grew hot, it would melt. Now on the sixth day they gathered twice as much bread, two omers for each one. When all the leaders of the congregation came and told Moses, then he said to them, "This is what the Lord meant: Tomorrow

is a sabbath observance, a holy sabbath to the Lord. Bake what you will bake and boil what you will boil, and all that is left over put aside to be kept until morning." So they put it aside until morning, as Moses had ordered, and it did not become foul nor was there any worm in it. Moses said, "Eat it today, for today is a sabbath to the Lord; today you will not find it in the field. "Six days you shall gather it, but on the seventh day, the sabbath, there will be none." It came about on the seventh day that some of the people went out to gather, but they found none. Then the Lord said to Moses, "How long do you refuse to keep My commandments and My instructions? See, the Lord has given you the sabbath; therefore He gives you bread for two days on the sixth day. Remain every man in his place; let no man go out of his place on the seventh day." So the people rested on the seventh day.

First of all, it is important to note that the command to observe the Sabbath comes before the giving of the Ten Commandments on Mount Sinai. While this might surprise some, it is perfectly rational since the nature of the Sabbath goes back to the establishment of creation. The command to keep the Sabbath, then, is restorative in nature. God seeks to restore the created order that was lost as a result of sin. All of creation was originally perfect and relied completely on God. The sin of Adam and Eve was a grasping for power, self-reliance, and independence from God, all qualities that stand in direct opposition to the nature of that first Sabbath.

Second, in the Exodus passage, the response of the Israelites to the command not to go out and gather manna on the Sabbath and God's ensuing disappointment specifically illustrates the core value of the Sabbath, which was only implied in the creation account: trust. God told the people not to go out and gather manna on the seventh day. He provided a double portion on the sixth day, and that portion did not decay as the extra manna had on other days. The Lord provided what they needed, just as he had in creation. But the people did not listen. Some still felt the need for control; they wanted to hedge their bets, so to speak. A little more work and some extra food stored would give them a sense of safety in their own provision. Fundamentally, they did not trust God. "How long do you refuse to keep My commandments and My instructions?" demands the Lord (Exod 16:28).[9] The Sabbath had come to represent a step toward a restored relationship with God and trust in him and his provision, but the people of Israel failed

9. Hebrew for "you" is plural at this point so God is addressing all the people.

even in this first step. The gulf between the Lord and his people remained, demonstrated in their inability to rest in his presence on the Sabbath.

The Sabbath command was formalized in the giving of the Ten Commandments in Exod 20 and the revisiting of these commandments in Deut 5. There are differences between Deuteronomy's version of the fourth commandment and that of Exodus, so we will look briefly at each. The Sabbath commandment is the lengthiest of all Ten Commandments in both versions. It serves as a pivot point between the first four and last six commandments. The first four focus on the relationship between us and God, whereas the last six center on our relationship with each other. In the fourth command, the Sabbath, all of these relationships come together.[10] In the Exodus version, the justification for keeping the Sabbath appears within the order of creation. Exod 20:8–11 (NASB) reads:

> Remember the sabbath day, to keep it holy. Six days you shall labor and do all your work, but the seventh day is a sabbath of the Lord your God; in it you shall not do any work, you or your son or your daughter, your male or your female servant or your cattle or your sojourner who stays with you. For in six days the Lord made the heavens and the earth, the sea and all that is in them, and rested on the seventh day; therefore the Lord blessed the sabbath day and made it holy.

Even as all of creation was finalized and rested with God on the seventh day, so too Israel, and all that was under their control and influence, was to rest with God on the seventh day. Keeping the Sabbath was to be part of the restoration of the created order. As Olson notes, it was also a reminder to the people that as God sanctified the Sabbath, he also sanctified them. The six days of creation served the purpose of enabling fellowship and rest with God. Sabbath was the sacred time in which creation fulfilled its purpose. So Israel was to *remember* their own purpose on the Sabbath, namely trusting in and fellowshipping with God. Just as the individual days of creation were incomplete in and of themselves, so was the work that Israel did during the other six days of the week. Their work did not sanctify them. God did. One day a week they were to *remember* this. One day of the week they were to practice complete trust in God as it was in the very beginning.

This same grounding in the order of creation is seen later in the book of Exodus. In 31:12–17 the Sabbath law is repeated following the instructions concerning the building of the six sections of the Tabernacle. These

---

10. See Olson, "Sacred Time," 5.

six sections represented a microcosm of creation. Even as creation was "built" in six days for the purpose of making fellowship between God and humanity possible, so too was the building of the six sections of the Tabernacle meant to lead to fellowship between God and Israel.[11] The purpose of the Tabernacle was to house the particular presence of God among the Israelites. Thus, in Exod 31 the sanctuary and the Sabbath were joined in purpose by God's presence. Sacred space and sacred time came together so that the Israelites could live in the presence of God. On a very small scale, the Sabbath and the Tabernacle represented the restoration of what was lost because of sin.

Deuteronomy and the Sabbath

Whereas Exodus looks back to creation for the justification for the Sabbath, Deuteronomy looks back to the redemption from Egypt and slavery. Deut 5:12–15 (NASB) states:

> Observe the sabbath day to keep it holy, as the Lord your God commanded you. Six days you shall labor and do all your work, but the seventh day is a sabbath of the Lord your God; in it you shall not do any work, you or your son or your daughter or your male servant or your female servant or your ox or your donkey or any of your cattle or your sojourner who stays with you, so that your male servant and your female servant may rest as well as you. You shall remember that you were a slave in the land of Egypt, and the Lord your God brought you out of there by a mighty hand and by an outstretched arm; therefore the Lord your God commanded you to observe the sabbath day.

It is worth noting that, while Exodus commands the people to *remember* the Sabbath, Deuteronomy commands that they *observe* or *keep* the Sabbath. Yet the importance of remembering is not lost in Deuteronomy's version. The reason that the people are to *observe* the Sabbath is so that they *remember* what it was like to be a slave in Egypt.[12] The command in Deuteronomy is based on the more recent experience of the generation who is about to enter the land of promise.[13] In Exodus the appeal to Sabbath-keeping is anchored in the trustworthy nature of God as evidenced in

11. Note a similar idea in Olson, "Sacred Time," 8.

12. Ibid., 17.

13. Novak, "The Sabbath Day," 73.

creation. In Deuteronomy, the same appeal finds grounding in the trust-worthy nature of God as evidenced in his redemptive activity and provision per the Exodus event. Both accounts tie the remembrance and observance of the Sabbath to the guarantee of God's provision. Indeed, resting on the Sabbath is very much tied to trusting in God as provider throughout the Pentateuch.

The ongoing relevance of the Sabbath, then, becomes associated with God's redemptive activity in saving the Israelites from captivity as well as God's provision in creation. As a result, the observation of the Sabbath is incumbent on the whole Israelite family. But Deuteronomy does not stop there: the Israelites are told that they are to treat those who are under their authority in the same manner as God treated them. The blessing of the Sabbath, rest due to trusting in God, is to be extended to the Gentiles who serve among the Israelites.[14] The Israelites knew from personal experience what it was like to be enslaved and to have no rest and no reprieve—when they complained to pharaoh in Egypt, their burden was increased.[15] When they cried out to God, they received deliverance. This deliverance was to be the model for their Sabbath praxis.

So we have seen that the command to observe Sabbath has its roots in the very character of God as Creator and Redeemer; he is a God who never changes. The natural human desire for control and self-oriented pleasure, however, does not fit well with Sabbath notions of rest. The resulting dis-satisfaction with Sabbath observance, and keeping the Torah in general, was something the prophets had to address.

Isaiah and the Sabbath

A couple of passages from Isaiah serve to illustrate the frustration of the people and the way they missed the point of the Torah generally, and thus the Sabbath in particular. During the divided kingdom of Israel and Judah, the people of both countries had adopted the customs of the surround-ing peoples and sought to manipulate God through ritual. As a result, Isa 1:10–13 condemns the people for going through the motions of reli-gious observance without any change in behavior or heart attitude. Rote

---

14. The Talmud speaks of relationships between Jews and Gentiles on the Sabbath and wrestles with how far to extend some of these blessings. E.g. Babylonian Talmud Gittin 61a.

15. Exod 5:10.

observance misses the intent of the Law.[16] The Torah was always intended to be a recipe for the outward behavior that reflected an inwardly humble heart for God. This is no less true for Sabbath observance. While we have seen the nature and origins of the Sabbath described in Genesis, Exodus, and Deuteronomy, it is Isa 58:13–14 (NASB) that explains how the people of God are to respond to the Sabbath. It reads:

> If because of the sabbath, you turn your foot from doing your own pleasure on My holy day, and call the sabbath a delight, the holy day of the Lord honorable, and honor it, desisting from your own ways, from seeking your own pleasure and speaking your own word, then you will take delight in the Lord, and I will make you ride on the heights of the earth; and I will feed you with the heritage of Jacob your father, for the mouth of the Lord has spoken.

Here we see the crux of the matter: the Sabbath is not a time to seek lesser pleasures in preference to God, but to seek him as the source of all delight.[17] The heart of the Sabbath is having joy in one's relationship with God. When we look back at the nature of the Sabbath in conjunction with creation and the redemption from Egypt, this idea makes perfect sense.

Because of this purpose, Isaiah notes the existence of the Sabbath in the new creation as well. Isaiah 66:23 (NASB) reads, "And it shall be from new moon to new moon And from sabbath to sabbath, All mankind will come to bow down before Me,' says the LORD." In the new creation, as in the original creation, all flesh will acknowledge God and the festivals and Sabbaths will be the marker for this event. All of creation will stop—one of the meanings of the Hebrew word *shabbat*—and acknowledge God and His perfection. Those who do not will be judged (Isa 66:24).[18]

Jesus's Teachings on Sabbath

The Old Testament teaches that the Sabbath is ongoing. Why do so many Christians believe that the Sabbath is the one commandment of the Ten that is null and void? Most often it is because of the assumption that Jesus abolished its observance in the New Testament with His statement that the "Son of Man is Lord of the Sabbath" (Matt 12:8 NASB). What did Jesus

16. E.g. Deut 10:12–16.

17. See also Isa 56:2–7.

18. This is derived from the larger context of Isa 66. See especially verses 18 and following.

mean by this particular statement? Was he really nullifying the Sabbath? To answer these questions we must take a closer look at the context of the surrounding verses and the cultural context in which it was spoken.[19]

At the beginning of Matt 12, Jesus and the disciples are walking in fields of grain and the disciples were picking grain and eating the kernels. Verse 1 is phrased very carefully to remind the contemporary audience that this was an acceptable activity according to Torah (Deut 23:25). The question presented to Jesus was whether or not this activity constituted forbidden work on the Sabbath. The exact parameters of what constituted work were a common point of debate at the time of Jesus, and he took the question seriously. At its core, after all, the question was born of a desire to be loyal to the commandments.[20] There were some activities that did override the Sabbath. For example, in John 7:22–23 Jesus notes that it was acceptable to perform a circumcision on the Sabbath even though cutting was normally forbidden on the Sabbath.[21] He argues this to show that he was still within the acceptable limits of observing the holy seventh day by healing someone.[22] In Matthew, Jesus answers the concerns of the Pharisees about picking grain with typical rabbinic argumentation. He notes how David and his men ate the consecrated bread that was meant only for the priests. The saving of David's life, however, overrode the prohibition against eating the consecrated bread. Jesus also notes the implication that the priests' preparation of the food on the Sabbath is in obedience to God's command, and therefore the priests who prepare the bread on the Sabbath are exempt and blameless of Sabbath violation.[23] This legal example leads Jesus to his concluding argument: the fact that he is greater than the temple. Since there were exceptions for Sabbath rules in relation to the temple, how much more would there be exceptions for the one who was greater than the temple?

Jesus then, quite literally, gets to the heart of the matter. He cites Hos 6:6 to illustrate that the heart of the Torah is more important than the literal command of the Torah. Verse 6 reveals God making this very point. Performing sacrifices perfectly with no heart for God or one's fellow Israelite

19. Jesus and his disciples faithfully attended synagogue. See Mark 1:21, Luke 13:10 and John 6:59.

20. Young, *Jesus*, 105.

21. Ibid., 106.

22. This argument is called a lesser to greater argument in rabbinic thought. In other words, if circumcision is permitted on the Sabbath, then how much more so should saving a life be permitted?

23. Talmud Shabbat, 15; Babylonian Talmud Yoma 85b.

was empty and meaningless. Just as the Israelites in Hosea were performing ritual with no heart for God, so the Pharisees had made the Sabbath a set of rules rather than the blessing of rest through fellowship with God. They had missed the heart of the Sabbath. As illustrated in the Old Testament passages, the purpose of the Sabbath was to be a sacred time in which needs are met and trust in God and fellowship with him are possible. Living in fellowship with Jesus and having their hunger satisfied was exactly what the disciples were doing.

The hinge of Matt 12 comes in verse 8: Jesus states that the Son of Man is Lord of the Sabbath. There are two possible interpretations to Jesus's meaning in this statement. In Ezekiel, the phrase "Son of Man" is used to indicate human frailty, whereas in Daniel it is used in association with deity. It seems more likely that, given the context of Jesus's claim to be greater than the temple, he is using the phrase to indicate his deity.[24] However, some sense of both frailty and deity may be in play, since Jesus is making the point that the Sabbath was made for the benefit of people and as a blessing of fellowship between people and God rather than a set of rules that must be kept without purpose. In Mark 2:27 (NASB), Jesus expresses it this way: "The Sabbath was made for man, and not man for the Sabbath."[25]

The verses after Matt 12:8 solidify this point when Jesus heals a man with a withered hand in the synagogue. Having a withered hand is not life-threatening in the same way that hunger may be. The Pharisees, therefore, questioned whether it was lawful to heal this particular man on the Sabbath. In this situation, Jesus again uses rabbinic argumentation. He points out that his critics would rescue one of their sheep that fell into a pit on the Sabbath, because it would be a good thing to do for the poor animal. Therefore, by extension, doing good to a man or woman is even more important, even if it means technically violating the Sabbath.

Christians often interpret this as a nullification of the Sabbath. This is not true, however. What is often missed by Christians in the teaching of Jesus is that he was very concerned with properly observing Sabbath and took the questions of the Pharisees seriously. Too often Christians are taught that the Pharisees were enemies and that Jesus completely rejected them

24. See Young, *Jesus*, 111, for the alternate position.

25. Mark 2:23—3:6 is the parallel passage to Matt 12. Interestingly, the statement about the priority of humanity over Sabbath was a common teaching in early rabbinic circles and was probably not unique to Jesus. He was tapping into well-known discussion points among the teachers of the time and taking a position in the common debate about what constituted lawful work on the Sabbath. See Young, *Jesus*, 108–9.

and their teachings. This was not the case, however. Jesus himself states, somewhat sarcastically, in Matt 23:3–4 that the Pharisees sit in the seat of Moses. Technically their teaching was correct and the disciples should listen to them, but should not follow in their inconsistent actions. Jesus was not nullifying the Sabbath. Lifting the heavy burdens of the Pharisees from Sabbath observance and emphasizing its purpose was not equivalent to eliminating its observance. Of course this leaves us with the question of what continued observance looks like. Before we can answer this question we must look at the writings of Paul and the book of Hebrews.

Paul's Writings and the Sabbath

While Jesus does endorse Sabbath observance with the proper attitude, many believers find a negation of the holy day for Christians in the words of Paul. There are three main passages in which Paul speaks about the Sabbath. The first of these is Rom 14:4–6, the well-known passage that addresses the issue of those who are weak in the faith. Paul mentions the observance of one day over another, but he does not specify the exact nature of the debate about days. Whether Paul is speaking about the Sabbath here or not is insignificant. His main point is that believers stay faithful in their heart to the Lord with respect to their activities. His primary concern is that people do not violate their conscience with actions brought about by outside pressure.

The second passage in which Paul may mention Sabbath is found in Gal 4:8–11. Here again the reference to Sabbath is implied only in his mention of observing certain days, months, and years. In this passage, Paul's focus is on the fact that observing special holy days or times cannot bring salvation. The people of Galatia apparently felt insecure about salvation by faith alone and started going back to ritual in order to secure their salvation. Paul sternly corrects them and reminds them that no ritual observance can save.

The final passage is in the same vein as the first two, but does mention the Sabbath specifically. In Col 2:14–17, Paul expounds on the salvific accomplishments of Jesus. He states that no one should judge another in terms of Sabbath observance. He does not forbid or endorse the observance of the Sabbath or other festivals. Instead, he states that all of the festivals found in the Old Testament were but shadows of the reality of what is to come and the substance of all things, including the Sabbath, is in the person of Jesus Christ. It is important to note that Paul is not rejecting the Sabbath.

In fact, it is best to understand this as an adoption of Jesus's explanation of the nature of Sabbath.

Hebrews and the Sabbath

Our last, and perhaps most important New Testament passage, is in Heb 3:15–4:13 (NASB). The passage reads:

> While it is said, "Today if you hear his voice, do not harden your hearts, as when they provoked me." For who provoked Him when they had heard? Indeed, did not all those who came out of Egypt led by Moses? And with whom was He angry for forty years? Was it not with those who sinned, whose bodies fell in the wilderness? And to whom did He swear that they would not enter His rest, but to those who were disobedient? So we see that they were not able to enter because of unbelief. Therefore, let us fear if, while a promise remains of entering His rest, any one of you may seem to have come short of it. For indeed we have had good news preached to us, just as they also; but the word they heard did not profit them, because it was not united by faith in those who heard. For we who have believed enter that rest, just as He has said, "As I swore in my wrath, they shall not enter my rest," although His works were finished from the foundation of the world. For He has said somewhere concerning the seventh day: "And God rested on the seventh day from all His works"; and again in this passage, "They shall not enter My rest." Therefore, since it remains for some to enter it, and those who formerly had good news preached to them failed to enter because of disobedience, He again fixes a certain day, "Today," saying through David after so long a time just as has been said before, "Today if you hear His voice, do not harden your hearts." For if Joshua had given them rest, He would not have spoken of another day after that. So there remains a Sabbath rest for the people of God. For the one who has entered His rest has himself also rested from his works, as God did from His. Therefore let us be diligent to enter that rest, so that no one will fall, through following the same example of disobedience. For the word of God is living and active and sharper than any two-edged sword, and piercing as far as the division of soul and spirit, of both joints and marrow, and able to judge the thoughts and intentions of the heart. And there is no creature hidden from His sight, but all things are open and laid bare to the eyes of Him with whom we have to do.

In this passage we have the clearest endorsement of the ongoing relevance for the Sabbath among the Christian community. The author of Hebrews couches his discussion in terms of obedience that leads to the Sabbath rest and, conversely, disobedience preventing that rest. The author is using a rabbinic argument to play on the word "rest" in Ps 95:11. In the psalm, God addresses the disobedience of the Israelites when they rebelled against Moses, Aaron, and God. This disobedience resulted in God's judgment: a whole generation would not enter into the land of Israel but instead would die in the wilderness. The writer of Hebrews understands that the Promised Land was to reflect the Garden of Eden on a smaller scale, as a place of restored fellowship between God and his people. Yet sin, hard hearts, and disobedience continued to bar the realization of this goal; and the same problem of rebellion bars the people of God from his rest.

At the center of this disobedience, according to Hebrews, is a lack of belief. The people did not trust God to meet all of their needs. They did not believe that they could rest in God. They had to maintain control because doubt about God's sufficiency gnawed at their belief. Just as it was in the Garden, the temptation to maintain control kept the Israelites from complete trust. Hebrews argues that since the command to trust in God and enter into his rest is anchored at creation, from the beginning of time, this command to give up control by resting in God's provision is still in effect as an indicator of belief. Indeed, the breaking or keeping of the Sabbath as a test of one's belief in God to provide is part of the prophetic message and is not original to Hebrews.[26] Even as faith without works is dead (Jas 2:20), so too is faith without resting in God's provision by ceasing from the activities that give us a sense of self-sufficiency. God himself set this standard at the end of creation. He subjected himself to time to illustrate where life has its focus. In this sense, Sabbath was a foreshadowing of the coming of Christ, who took on time and flesh to show what complete trust and rest, *shalom*, looked like among the faithful.[27] We can see this fulfillment when his disciples pluck grain and have their needs met while focusing on fellowship with Jesus. We see God's provision when Jesus heals on the Sabbath. We even see a complete trust in God in his submission to the cross, the ultimate act of faith. For the author of Hebrews Sabbath keeping is still an active command. Entering into Sabbath rest is the ultimate test of a genuine faith.

---

26. Isa 56:4; Ezek 20:12–13, 16, 20–21, 24; 22:8, 26; Amos 8:4–5.

27. Olson, "Sacred Time," 13.

Conclusion: The Sabbath Today

How then does Sabbath apply to us today? How does it fit in with our busy, hectic lives? Should we be resting for 24 hours on Saturday or Sunday? One conclusion we can draw from the teachings of Paul and Hebrews is that the 24-hour cycle does not seem to be binding on believers in Jesus in the same way that it was on the Jews of Jesus's time. Yet, the New Testament does view the principles of Sabbath found in the Old Testament to remain binding in some sense. We cannot jettison the fourth commandment without good reason, and such a reason does not exist in the Bible. However, Jesus and Paul indicate that the type of observance carried out by some of the Pharisees and those who sought salvation in ritual was meaningless to God.

As we have seen, the positive aspects of keeping Sabbath that are found in the New Testament accurately reflect the intention of Sabbath in the Old Testament. From the very beginning, Sabbath was a point in time in which God demonstrated complete and perfect provision. He was a God who could be trusted and relied upon to provide so that people could fellowship with him. The primary purpose of creation and humanity was to fellowship with God in complete trust. From the fall into sin, however, humanity has failed time and again to believe that God is trustworthy. At the core, our own concerns and drive toward endless work end up being a desire for control of our own world. The command to keep Sabbath and remember where we come from is a command to let our desire for control go and trust God so completely that we are able to rest in the security and fellowship we find with him. Hebrews notes that this command continues. God has continued to be faithful. Jesus demonstrated faithfulness and trust in God to the point of death for us on the cross and God's trustworthiness in the resurrection. Hebrews warns that failure to enter into the Sabbath rest and trust in God's provision is to commit the same sin that affected the Israelites—disobedience through unbelief.

The primary focus of the Sabbath, then, is on our relationship with God and being able to fully trust him. Yet, as we see throughout the Bible, there is also an emphasis on how we interact with others on the Sabbath. The very nature of Sabbath precludes the possibility of selfishness on that holy day. The Old Testament speaks of extending the blessing of Sabbath to the foreigners who live with the people of God and serve them during the week. Jesus speaks of doing good for others and anything that would save a life as part of Sabbath observance. We cannot say we have a genuine relationship with God while turning a blind eye to the needs of others.

Sabbath requires full commitment to God and His creation if we are truly to honor it.

But does this mean that we need to observe a single day in a particularly ritualistic way? Not necessarily, but the Sabbath today needs to be long enough to get our attention. As theologian Marguerite Shuster notes, "Beliefs cut off from practices tend to become vacuous."[28] In a very real manner, this is what has happened with the Sabbath in the modern church. Since we no longer consciously practice a Sabbath, we no longer think about what it means for us and our relationship with God. Ironically, it is the exact opposite problem from the time of the New Testament, during which practice had become more important than belief. Both practice and belief must be wedded together and neither can be discarded without eroding the principle of keeping the Sabbath. In other words, we do need to observe the Sabbath in some practical way and we need to understand the heart impact that the observance is meant to produce. We must consciously let go of our desire for control and rest in the trustworthiness of God's provision.

Yet this remains for us one of the most difficult commands in Scripture to keep. Shuster explains, "We worry about the costs of stopping that we can count; we ignore the costs of not stopping, for we do not know how to count them. We are afraid to trust in a world that seems arbitrary and erratic at best; we ignore the fact that all we do assumes a trust in the existence and regularities of a creation not under our control."[29] As a result, "We are ready to mouth truths about the Lord's claim upon our lives, yet reluctant to give the Lord exclusive claim upon a single day of the week."[30] While the New Testament does not seem to require observance of a single day of the week for believers, it is actually more demanding. Hebrews especially calls for entering into a Sabbath rest that is defined by complete faith and obedience in God and implies that this kind of trust should be a lifestyle rather than a once a week observance. This sort of lifestyle of complete surrender to God is so foreign to us and our hectic lifestyles that the reality is that we barely give it one to two hours on Sunday mornings in our culture.

If one day a week is not required, but a so-called lifestyle is, practically speaking, how do we observe and benefit from the Sabbath? There is no doubt that believers would benefit from deliberately setting aside one day a week to consciously seek God and rest in him. As noted above, many of

28. Shuster, "Response, 83."
29. Ibid.
30. Ibid., 85.

the festivals in the Old Testament are shadows of things fulfilled in the New Testament. This is the case with the Sabbath as well. The Old Testament requires actively giving up the original sin of grasping for control and resting in God once a week. The New Testament calls us to rest in God every moment of our lives. However, limited human nature is unable to make lifestyle changes quickly. Those who are addicted to cigarettes are rarely able to quit overnight. They have to do it in stages. Keeping the heart principle of Sabbath is an even greater challenge. Therefore, most of us, who are hooked on a life of constant activity, and making sure our world is under our control, will have to learn to keep the Sabbath principles in stages.

Practicing Sabbath may very well take different forms for different believers, and the New Testament allows for just such an arrangement. Perhaps the simple act of turning off your cell phone for a day would represent the beginning of entering God's rest. Acknowledging that God is in control and that you can be off the grid for one day in order to focus on God and His provision may be where you need to start. Hopefully this simple practice will spill into the rest of the week in terms of your need for control via being available all the time. When you start to become stressed about important calls you will remember the Sabbath and Who is really in control. You will trust in his care for you and, as a result, you will enter his rest.

You may have other areas in your life that you feel you must control and you cannot let them go for even one day a week, let alone the whole week. Maybe it is paperwork or paying bills. Maybe it is watching television or housecleaning. Some things we will gladly give up for a day a week or for the whole week, if we could get away with it. However, giving things up because we do not want to do them does not count. More than likely there are a number of things that represent our unwillingness to trust God completely and we may need to focus on several of them for one day a week as a start. Sabbath challenges us to identify these areas for what they are: a lack of belief that God can really take care of everything. Therefore, the activities that we give up should reflect pressure points in our lives, places where we struggle to trust God to provide. Ideally, the practice of trusting and resting in God for one day a week will become a lifestyle so that you no longer feel the driving need to control your own world.

For all of us, a dedicated time with other believers praying and studying Scripture should certainly play a role in keeping the principle of Sabbath. The key is a focus on God and surrendering to him, and this is not an act that is always done in solitude. Fellowship with God often involves fellowship with others. Again, starting with one day a week, we can intentionally focus on what God has done for us and extend that blessing to others. The example here comes from Jesus. Whenever he did something that "violated" the Sabbath, he did it to alleviate a need that kept someone from fully enjoying fellowship with God. The focus should be on intentionally letting God use us to help others trust in his provision.

The act of consciously putting your faith in God's provision and letting that faith govern your actions for one day a week is the place to start. As Abraham Heschel notes, "Six days a week we seek to dominate the world, on the seventh day we try to dominate the self."[31] Hopefully, the attitude of submission that is cultivated during these Sabbath days will begin to spill into other days of the week. Edmund Clowney states it well: "By marking out that day, God's children are reminded that they belong to God as physical creatures and depend on him for their very breath. They are also reminded that their purpose is not the labor itself so much as it is their communion with the God who made them."[32] In the face of our busy world and lives, we can practice Sabbath by trusting in God and his provision one day a week with the intention that this will become a pattern that reflects our belief every day.

31. Heschel, *The Sabbath*, 13. Heschel may mean this with respect to our own power, but I would understand the need to dominate the self to take on the form of submission to God.

32. Clowney, *How Jesus Transforms*, 55.

2

Fair Trade

What Would Jesus Drink?[1]

RUSSELL L. MEEK AND WILLIAM K. BECHTOLD

Introduction

JORGE IS A SOUTH American coffee farmer who works sixteen-hour days to support his family, but he soon realizes there are not enough hours in the week to provide a living for them. He knows that people across the world drink coffee from farms like his, yet he cannot support his family because the importers who buy his coffee beans refuse to pay him an appropriate price for it. Rather than sharing with Jorge the earnings from selling his coffee, the importers pocket exorbitant profits. Unfortunately, Jorge has little choice in the matter because he can either sell his coffee at a price too low to provide for his family, or not sell at all. He does not have the option to sell his coffee at the higher price that Fair Trade guarantees because consumers refuse to pay more per pound for their coffee. Because of this, he is caught in a perpetual cycle of poverty that will only be broken when we consumers choose to use our purchasing power for the benefit of the producers.

A common objection to Jorge's situation is "This is the free market, and that is how things work." However, in this essay we will paint a picture

1. The authors would like to thank Matthew Arbo and Blake Hearson for their insightful comments regarding this issue of Fair Trade. Any errors remain our own.

of how the market *could* work for Jorge. We will examine the issue of Fair Trade and suggest that, as Christians, we should pay higher prices in exchange for contributing to the well-being of other humans across the globe. Rather than protecting our wallets, we propose that we should purchase our coffee and other products at a higher price to ensure that Jorge, and the untold millions like him, gets a living wage for his work. After all, "the laborer deserves his wages" (Luke 10:7 ESV).

In order to make the case that Christians should engage in conscientious consumption, this chapter addresses the issue of Fair Trade first by briefly explaining what Fair Trade is and whom it benefits. We then look at the biblical mandate to care for the poor, which we argue obligates Christians to engage in fair trading practices. We understand that Fair Trade is an enormous issue, as is the role of Christians in a world economy. Therefore, we necessarily only scratch the surface of these issues, leaving much of the nuance of the discussion to others. We recognize that there is no perfect solution; nevertheless, we feel it is important to call Christians to help the poor by taking the small step of purchasing their coffee, tea, chocolate, and other commodities from those who offer a living wage to the producers of these beloved products.

What is Fair Trade?

Fair Trade is a term used to indicate goods that an external organization certified as meeting certain conditions and that were purchased at a price that provides a living wage, regardless of the market price.[2] This means that even if the market price for green coffee is $.50 per pound, Fair Trade importers purchase the coffee for the $1.25 per pound that ensures a suitable standard of living for the workers responsible for growing and harvesting the coffee. The higher purchasing price explains the higher sticker price at the store.

---

2. An ideal solution to the issue of fair trade will take into consideration the fact that living wages vary from region to region and adjust the price of Fair Trade products accordingly.

Fair Trade Parties[3]

In order for Fair Trade to be effective, three parties must be involved. First, the producers—those who grow or make the products—must be committed to Fair Trade practices. Second, the importers—those who purchase the goods from the producers—must be committed to paying a higher price for goods they could purchase elsewhere for less. Finally, the consumers—people like us—must be committed to spending just a bit more for our coffee and other goods to ensure that the first group of people—producers such as Jorge—can earn a living wage. We realize that in the Western world in this century it is well nigh impossible to purchase *only* Fair Trade products. This would require a radical reorganization of the entire world economy. However, while we can do relatively little to impact the world economy, we *can* make the decision to purchase our products only from organizations committed to Fair Trade, thus making a difference (however small) where we are.[4]

Certification of Fair Trade Products

In order to advertise one's products as "Fair Trade," importers must be certified by another organization that sets standards for Fair Trade products, such as the International Federation for Alternative Trade (IFAT) or the Fairtrade Labeling Organization International (FLO). Simply put, in order to qualify as Fair Trade, the importers must pay a price high enough to cover the producers' cost of living, as well as contribute to the social and economic development of the region as a whole.[5] The importers must also commit to long-term contracts, which gives producers the stability needed to refuse selling their product at a lower price to non-Fair Trade importers.[6] On the production end, the workers must be organized democratically (similar to unions in the United States), and the employers must provide benefits, fair wages, safe working conditions, and equal treatment along

---

3. See World Centric, "Fair Trade?" para. 4–6.

4. While this essay deals primarily with luxury goods such as coffee and chocolate, the best possible scenario is one in which *all* goods are bought and sold ethically, that is, in a way that ensures that no exploitation of others occurs.

5. Ibid., para. 8.

6. Ibid, para. 7. See also Brown, *Fair Trade*, 164.

gender lines.[7] Furthermore, producers must produce evidence that the money they receive is actually passed along to the workers.[8] This system is meant to ensure that when we purchase Fair Trade goods we can be certain that we are contributing to the betterment of fellow human beings rather than enjoying goods at their expense.

Problems and Benefits of Fair Trade

Problems with Fair Trade

Fair Trade provides an avenue for consumption of goods that prevents exploitation, but it is not flawless. First, the certification process is costly and burdensome for small producers who are already battling poverty.[9] Second, once organizations receive Fair Trade certification, they can claim to engage in Fair Trade regardless of how many of their products are Fair Trade certified.[10] For example, if a company purchases only ten percent of its coffee through Fair Trade agreements, that company can claim Fair Trade without disclosing to the public that only a minority of its products are actually traded fairly. Such lack of transparency can lead to confusion among consumers who want to purchase Fair Trade products, but who are not aware that companies do not have to engage in Fair Trade all of the time. In order to rectify this situation, there needs to be a way to differentiate between those companies who practice ethical trading all of the time and those who do not.[11] Third, by purchasing fairly traded goods, the consumer is spending more money on less product, which could cause a decrease in the demand of the product. This can have the unintended consequence of creating a glut in the market, which leads to unsold products.

Benefits of Fair Trade

The benefits of Fair Trade for the consumer have little to do with money. In fact, by purchasing Fair Trade products, we will be spending *more* money than if we simply shopped around for the best deal. However, our financial

7. Moore, "Fair Trade Movement," 79. See also World Centric, "Fair Trade?," para. 10.
8. Ibid.
9. Ibid., para. 12.
10. Ibid., para. 13–15.
11. Ibid. See also Moore, "Fair Trade Movement," 82–83.

loss is gain for the people on the other side of the world who provide the products that we love to consume. The benefits for the consumer, then, are significantly greater than the financial cost associated with Fair Trade.

A significant benefit of purchasing Fair Trade products is that it enables us to take responsibility for the purchasing choices we make. By taking the simple step of drinking Fair Trade coffee or eating Fair Trade chocolate, we can know that we are supporting the global community. Rather than being a part of the problem that comes with unfair trade practices, such as the exploitation of others (including children), we can be part of the solution. Furthermore, by engaging in Fair Trade, we are saying with our wallets that people are more important than products.[12] When given a choice, who wouldn't want to ensure that their purchases enhanced the lives of other people?

Christians especially must be attuned to how we live our lives. Our verbal proclamation of the gospel should be accompanied by godly living, which includes the protection of the poor. The Bible does not explicitly address Fair Trade, but it does set strict guidelines for believers regarding treatment of the poor and less fortunate. These texts apply to the issue of Fair Trade because the heart of Fair Trade is caring for the poor by offering them a way to support themselves.

The evangelical response to Fair Trade must therefore be based on the biblical standard for the treatment of the poor, not simply a discussion of the potential benefits of Fair Trade. The rest of the essay will outline that standard from an overview of both Old and New Testament theology. We recognize that the Bible originally spoke in a different cultural and historical context that had not been confronted with Fair Trade. Nevertheless, several relevant principles speak to the issues of the poor and Fair Trade. Our position is that biblical theology of the poor puts a strong burden on the people of God—a burden that should outweigh many of the problems with Fair Trade outlined above, especially any material concerns. The weight of the biblical evidence is compelling—a higher sticker price is insignificant when weighed against the responsibility God's people bear for just treatment of the poor.

---

12. Brown forcefully argues that we *must* adopt a different lifestyle for the betterment of the rest of the world (*Fair Trade*, 177–9).

The Poor in the Old Testament

The Poor and the Law

Right treatment of the poor (along with widows and orphans) plays a prominent role in the law codes established in the Old Testament Pentateuch (Genesis–Deuteronomy). Even before the law at Sinai (and again at Moab), God had established that each human was endowed with an innate dignity: "Whoever spills the blood of man, by man his blood will be spilled. For in the image of God he made man" (Gen 9:6 NASB). This first pronouncement after the flood reaffirmed humanity's place above all other creatures (cf. Gen. 1:26–30) and established the death penalty for murder. As God's image-bearers, all people are responsible to one another. This detail is vital—the poor worker barely scraping a living half a world away bears as much of God's image as a minister preaching the gospel in our church every week.

As one would expect, God's laws place a high premium on treatment of oft-afflicted groups such as slaves, women, widows, orphans, and foreigners, and he holds his people to a high standard in their responsibility toward those groups. As Bruce Malchow writes, "The commands prohibit oppressive actions and call for positive deeds toward the deprived."[13] In the Book of the Covenant (Exod 20:22–23:33)—nestled among such evangelical mainstays as restrictions against witchcraft (Exod 22:18), bestiality (Exod 22:19), and polytheism (Exod 22:20)—mistreatment of the foreigner is strictly forbidden: "You shall not wrong a stranger or oppress him, for you were strangers in the land of Egypt" (Exod 22:21 NASB; cf. 23:9). Restrictions against the mistreatment of widows and orphans (Exod 22:22–23) and restrictions against charging interest when lending money to the poor among God's people (Exod 22:25–27) follow the command to treat the foreigner well. Strong words reinforce these concerns: "You shall not afflict any widow or orphan. If you afflict him at all, and if he does cry out to me, I will surely hear his cry and My anger will be kindled, and I will kill you with the sword, and your wives shall become widows and your children fatherless" (Exod 22:22–24 NASB; cf. v. 26–27). The implication is clear: the Lord is not indifferent to the plight of the misfortunate and his people are to emulate him by responding likewise. The Lord speaks and acts as if he has a vested interest in the welfare of the poor, and the cries of the oppressed do not fall on deaf ears.

13. Malchow, "Social Justice," 302. This section is indebted to Malchow's work.

The Holiness Code of Leviticus (Lev 17–26) expresses similar concern for the poor. Leviticus already provided the opportunity for the poor to bring a less expensive sacrifice (Lev 12:8; 14:21–22), and the Holiness Code builds on this concern, commanding that harvesters leave fallen fruit for the poor (Lev 19:10; 23:22). In Lev 19:33–34 (NASB) we find an echo of Exod 22:21: "When a stranger resides with you in your land, you shall not do him wrong. The stranger who resides with you shall be to you as the native among you, and you shall love him as yourself, for you were aliens in the land of Egypt; I am the Lord your God."[14] The poor of Israel were to be supported, not exploited for profit (Lev 25:35–37). Further, they could not serve as indentured servants permanently, but were to be released during the year of Jubilee (Lev 25:39–43).

Deuteronomy has similar laws concerning right treatment of the foreigner (Deut 10:19), fair weights (Deut 25:13–15), and the perversion of justice against less fortunate groups (Deut 24:17), along with the provision that these groups be allowed the portion of the harvest left behind (Deut 24:19–22), and protection against having their home invaded by a "bill collector" (Deut 24:10–11). Perhaps most striking are the words of Deut 15:7–11 (NASB):

> If there is a poor man with you, one of your brothers, in any of your towns in your land which the Lord your God is giving you, you shall not harden your hearts, nor close your hand from your poor brother; but you shall freely open your hand to him, and shall generously lend him sufficient for his need in whatever he lacks. Beware that there is no base thought in your heart, saying, "The seventh year, the year of remission, is near," and your eye is hostile toward your brother, and you give him nothing; then he may cry to the Lord against you, and it will be a sin in you. You shall generously give to him, and your heart shall not be grieved when you give to him, because for this thing the LORD your God will bless you in all your work and in all your undertakings. For the poor will never cease to be in the land; therefore I command you, saying, "You shall freely open your hand to your brother, to your needy and poor in your land."

This places a clear standard on the people of God: they are to care for the poor *willingly*, regardless of whether the poor will be able to pay back the debt (i.e., that the year of remission would come and cancel the debt). The

---

14. Is it too much to wonder just what impact verses like these should have on the evangelical response to the immigration debate in the United States?

burden of provision is on the people, not on the poor, and failure to provide for their needs—whatever they are—results in sin.

What do we learn from these law codes? First, God shows a special concern for certain groups of "unfortunates": the poor, widows, orphans, and foreigners. Second, God's people had an explicit responsibility to care for the poor (along with the other unfortunates). Third, these groups were not required to meet any special conditions to qualify for such treatment—the Lord simply showed them his concern.

We find no injunction for the poor to work their way out of their condition. While such a burden on the wealthy may be called unfair by modern standards, the Pentateuch shows no such concern. That there would be poor in the land is assumed (Deut 15:11), and Israel was to treat the poor well and provide for their needs, whatever they might be. Perhaps most relevant to our present discussion is the promise that mistreatment of these groups will not go unnoticed by God. Their prayers are given special mention (e.g. Exod 22:22–23), and the Lord leaves no doubt that he is on their side.

The Poor in the Prophets

The Prophets reminded the people of their covenant expectations, including their responsibilities to the poor. Faithfulness to the covenant meant more than right ritual—though this did not escape the fierce gaze of the prophets (cf. Jer 7:16–19; Mal 1:6–14)—it meant right behavior toward others. These two concerns—worship and ethics—show up most clearly in the Ten Commandments: the first four treating the former relationship, and the final six treating the latter relationship. The prophets clearly expect right treatment of others as key elements of Israel's (and Judah's) covenant responsibilities, as our brief examination will show.

Righteous worship went hand-in-hand with just conduct, as Micah makes clear in his famous oracle. He asks rhetorically, "With what shall I come to the Lord and bow myself before the God on high? Shall I come to Him with burnt offerings, with yearling calves?" (Mic 6:6 NASB). The answer: "He has told you, O man, what is good; and what does the Lord require of you but to do justice, to love kindness, and to walk humbly with your God?" (Mic 6:8 NASB). In the words of R. D. Patterson, "True righteousness, a living relationship with the Lord, would be evidenced in a type of conduct that reflected His high ethical standards."[15] A similar concern is found in Isa 58:6–12 (NASB):

> Is this not the fast which I choose, to loosen the bonds of wickedness, to undo the bands of the yoke, and to the let the oppressed go free and break every yoke? Is it not to divide your bread with the hungry and bring the homeless poor into the house; when you see the naked, to cover him; and not to hide yourself from your own flesh? Then your light will break out like the dawn, and your recovery will speedily spring forth; and your righteousness will go before you; the glory of the Lord will be your rear guard. Then you will call, and the Lord will answer; you will cry, and He will say, "Here I am." If you remove the yoke from your midst, the point of the finger and speaking wickedness; and if you give yourself to the hungry and satisfy the desire of the afflicted, then your light will rise in the darkness and your gloom will become like midday.

The expectation here is clearly the right treatment of the poor—justice and provision—and is more important than a rote (and perhaps grudging) devotion to the system of sacrifice because just actions demonstrate true worship.

The book of Amos provides an object lesson in how God's people were held accountable to the covenantal standard of justice and righteousness. His cry is against a people who have perverted both justice and righteousness, calling out against "those who turn justice into wormwood and cast righteousness down to the earth" (Amos 5:7 NASB). Among his indictments are poignant images of a people too intent on wallowing in luxury to treat the poor appropriately. For example, in Amos 2:6–8 (NASB), we read this:

> Thus says the Lord, "For three transgression of Israel and for four I will not revoke its punishment, because they sell the righteous for money and the needy for a pair of sandals. Those who pant after the very dust of the earth on the head of the helpless also turn aside the way of the humble; and a man and his father resort to the same girl in order to profane My holy name. On garments taken as pledges they stretch out beside every altar, and in the house of their God they drink the wine of those who have been fined."

Similarly, we read in Amos 5:11–12 (NASB):

---

15. Patterson, "The Widow, the Orphan, and the Poor," 231.

> Therefore because you impose heavy rent on the poor and exact a
> tribute of grain from them, though you have built houses of well-
> hewn stone, yet you will not live in them; you have planted pleas-
> ant vineyards, yet you will not drink their wine. For I know your
> transgressions are many and your sins are great, you who distress
> the righteous and accept bribes and turn aside the poor in the gate.

Amos condemns Israel for their treatment of the poor. They care more for
things than for the welfare of the needy, going so far as to sell poor people
into slavery (Amos 2:6). Israel worships in the house of God while abusing
the poor (Amos 2:8). They take necessities from the poor to build luxuries
for themselves (Amos 5:11), ultimately ignoring the needy at the very gates
to the city, where people would come to find justice (Amos 5:12). Such
behavior cannot be tolerated, and the luxuries built while oppressing the
poor will be taken away (Amos 5:11).

Most relevant to our topic are the words of Amos 4:1 (NASB), "Hear
this word, you cows of Bashan who are on the mountain of Samaria, who
oppress the poor, who crush the needy, who say to your husbands, 'Bring
now, that we may drink!'" Here, stately women call upon their husbands
to increase their own luxuries, all the while oppressing and crushing the
needy. Such "cows" give no thought to the plight of the poor; their eyes are
on themselves and their comfort. There can be no doubt about the Lord's
attitude concerning such callous attitudes: "the Lord God has sworn by His
holiness that, behold, days are coming upon you when you will be taken
with hooks—every last one of you with fishhooks" (Amos 4:2).[16]

The book of Amos presents a cautionary tale. The Lord demands
justice and righteousness, and does not tolerate mistreatment of the poor,
especially when reinforced with an insensitive devotion to one's own material splendor. The people of God have a responsibility to social justice.
When material gain is more highly valued than those in need, justice is
perverted. When the needy are crushed and the people of God turn a blind
eye—looking instead to their own wealth and their own indulgences—God
is not blind.

It is clear that the Old Testament places a high priority on right treatment of the poor. Before moving on to the New Testament, we should
in passing mention that *all three* sections (in the traditional sense: Law,
Prophets, Writings) of the Old Testament devote space to this concern.
Indeed, no fewer than fifteen individual Proverbs address right treatment

---

16. Translation is the authors' own.

of the poor.[17] We do not have the space to list them all, but mention only a couple as way of illustration. Proverbs 14:31 (NASB cf. 17:5) reads: "He who oppresses the poor taunts his Maker, but he who is gracious to the needy honors Him." In Prov 22:16 (NASB), we find words quite appropriate to our topic: "He who oppresses the poor to make more for himself or gives to the rich will only come to poverty."

The Poor in the New Testament

The New Testament is no less demanding regarding the responsibility of God's people to the poor and marginalized. As with many Old Testament concepts, Jesus takes the believer's duty toward his brother and makes it about more than outward action. "This is My commandment," he tells his disciples, "that you love one another, just as I have loved you. Greater love has no one than this, that one lay down his life for his friends. You are my friends if you do what I command you" (John 15:12–14 NASB). A central component of the disciple's life is humility, not only before God, but also before others. Their good becomes his good. This is not new, but a summary of the requirements of the law (Mark 12:28–31). Jesus himself demonstrated this principle in his own life by loving and caring for the needs of all kinds of people: prostitutes, tax collectors, Roman occupiers, those who were crucifying and mocking him, and even a disciple who had denied him. Jesus's attitude was one of humility; he did not cling to his rights or his riches, but emptied himself for the sake of others; and his loss was not only material possessions, but he became "obedient to the point of death, even death on a cross" (Phil 2:8 NASB). Christ's church is to have the same attitude, which means that we are to "not merely look out for your own personal interests, but also for the interests of others" (Phil 2:4 NASB). As we examine the New Testament principles of how we are to treat the poor, this single principle is the foundation on which all others are built: we are to put the good of others before ourselves because in so doing we not only follow the example of Christ, but also show that we are truly disciples of the One we call Lord.

17. E.g. Prov 13:23; 14:21; 14:31; 16:19; 17:5; 19:17; 21:13; 22:2; 22:16; 28:27; 29:7; 29:14; 30:14; 31:9; 31:20.

Jesus and the Poor[18]

In the Sermon on the Mount, Jesus takes for granted that his disciples would give to the poor (Matt 6:2–4), and even commands self-sacrificing giving: "Give to the one who begs from you, and do not refuse the one who would borrow from you" (Matt 5:42 NASB). Indeed, such giving should be done with no expectation of repayment (Luke 6:35). In Jesus's theology, as in that of the Old Testament Prophets, faithfulness to one's "religious" duties goes hand-in-hand with faithfulness to one's neighbor, as demonstrated in Matt 5:23–24 (NASB): "Therefore if you are presenting your offering at the altar, and there remember that your brother has something against you, leave your offering there before the altar and go, first be reconciled to your brother, and then come and present your offering."

More specifically, our religious duties cannot take the place of our responsibilities to others: "But you say, 'Whoever says to his father or mother, "Whatever I have that would help you has been given to God," he is not to honor his father or his mother.' And by this you invalidated the word of God for the sake of your tradition" (Matt 15:5–6 NASB; cf. Mark 7:11). Mark 12:38–40 (NASB) echoes this rebuke: "Beware of the scribes who like to walk around in long robes, and like respectful greetings in the market places, and chief seats in the synagogues, and places of honor at banquets, who devour widows' houses, and for appearance's sake offer long prayers; these will receive greater condemnation." Keeping up religious appearances is worthless when it accompanies injustice and pride.

The interaction in Matt 19:16–26 (cf. Mark 10:17–31) shows both Jesus's attitude toward material possessions and the attitude his disciples must have in following him. When a rich young man questioned Jesus on how to obtain eternal life, claiming to have kept the law (Matt 19:20), Jesus answered him, "If you wish to be complete, go and sell your possessions and give to the poor, and you will have treasure in heaven; and come follow me" (Matt 19:21 NASB). The young man went away dejected, "for he was one who owned much property" (Matt 19:22 NASB). The lesson of this passage is not that we are required to sell all of our possessions, but that we must be *willing* to give up those possessions for the sake of following Christ. While the young man claimed to have kept the law (and notice that when Jesus outlines those elements of the law he must keep, he lists

18. This section is indebted to research done in the following works: Beavis, "'Expecting Nothing in Return,'" 357–68; Blomberg, "Give Me neither Poverty nor Riches," 209–26; Snodgrass, "Jesus and Money," 135–43.

only the interpersonal ones—Matt 19:18–19), by loving his own possessions more than he loved others (i.e., the poor) the young man showed that he had truly not kept the law. Wealth's allure, when it distracts from our responsibility to care for others, ultimately distracts from our faithfulness to God. Thus, Jesus's words: "Again, I say to you, it is easier for a camel to go through the eye of a needle than for a rich man to enter the kingdom of God" (Matt 19:24 NASB). Matthew 6:19 (NASB) reiterates this attitude: "Do not store up for yourselves treasure on earth, where moth and rust destroy, and where thieves break in and steal."

Ultimately, we should place Jesus before us as an example of how we should think of the poor. He quoted Isaiah to introduce his ministry in Nazareth: "The Spirit of the Lord is upon me, because He anointed me to preach the gospel to the poor" (Luke 4:18 NASB). Further, we should take heart of Luke's account of our Lord's beatitudes: "Blessed are you who are poor, for yours is the kingdom of God. Blessed are you who hunger now, for you shall be satisfied" (Luke 6:20–21 NASB). With Jesus as our example, it is clear what our attitude toward the poor should be. In the words of Klyne Snodgrass, "We cannot claim to follow Jesus and not care about the poor or hide from the poor, which our neighborhoods often allow. If it is nothing else, the gospel of Jesus is good news for the poor."[19]

While this has been only a brief exploration of Jesus's teaching concerning the poor, it demonstrates two principles: 1) selfless treatment of others is a key religious duty for Jesus's disciples; 2) it is imperative that we value others more than we value the accumulation and maintenance of wealth. Such an attitude is reflected in the early church as described in Acts 4:32 (NASB): "And the congregation of those who believed were of one heart and soul; and not one of them claimed that anything belonging to him was his own, but all things were common property to them." This passage is perhaps more descriptive than prescriptive, but as disciples of Jesus we would be well-served by reflecting on its implications in our lives, especially in light of the teaching of the One we call Lord.

The Poor in the Epistles

As would be expected, the epistles reinforce Jesus's commands and examples regarding treatment of the poor. We noted above Paul's words to the Philippians concerning emulating Christ's selfless attitude. Such an attitude

19. Snodgrass, "Jesus and Money," 143.

would certainly be extended toward the poor. As Paul reminds the Galatians, when he was accepted by council of Jerusalem "They [James, Peter, and John] only asked us to remember the poor—the very thing I also was eager to do" (Gal 2:10 NASB). To the Romans, he cites the generous contribution for the poor in Jerusalem that the saints of Macedonia and Achaia made, "Yes, they were pleased to do so, and they are indebted to them. For if the Gentiles have shared in their spiritual things, they are indebted to minister to them also in material things" (Rom 15:27 NASB). These examples show the concern the first-century church had for the poor among them, and that such concern did not stop at any borders.

Care for the unfortunate was not simply a characteristic of the early church; it was expected of them. Paul writes to the Thessalonians: "We urge you, brethren, admonish the unruly, encourage the fainthearted, help the weak, be patient with everyone. See that no one repays another with evil for evil, but always seek after that which is good for one another and for all people" (1 Thess 5:14–15 NASB). John writes these words in his first epistle, "But whoever has the world's goods, and sees his brother in need and closes his heart against him, how does the love of God abide in him?" (1 John 3:17 NASB). The lesson is clear—those who have are to help those who have not, thereby demonstrating God's abiding love.

James's epistle provides perhaps the most appropriate material for our study here. Like the Old Testament prophets, he exhorts his readers, stating that, "Pure and undefiled religion in the sight of our God and Father is this: to visit orphans and widows in their distress, and to keep oneself unstained by the world" (Jas 1:27 NASB). Again, we are reminded of the interpersonal responsibility the Christian religion requires toward the unfortunate. James provides appropriate perspective for both the rich and the poor, "Listen, my beloved brethren: did not God choose the poor of this world to be rich in faith and heirs of the kingdom which he promised to those who love Him? But you have dishonored the poor man. Is it not the rich who oppress you and personally drag you into court? Do they not blaspheme the fair name by which you have been called?" (Jas 2:5–7 NASB; cf. 1:9–11). Though these words come in the midst of a discussion about special treatment for the rich, it illustrates the place of the poor in the gospel. Finally, and quite appropriately, James 5 contains these strong words,

> Come now, you rich, weep and howl for your miseries which are coming upon you. Your riches have rotted and your garments have become moth-eaten. Your gold and your silver have rusted; and

their rust will be a witness against you and will consume your flesh like fire. It is in the last days that you have stored up your treasure! Behold, the pay of the laborers who mowed your fields, and which has been withheld by you, cries out against you; and the outcry of those who did the harvesting has reached the ears of the Lord of Sabaoth. You have lived luxuriously on the earth and led a life of wanton pleasure; you have fattened your hearts in a day of slaughter. You have condemned and put to death the righteous man; he does not resist you (James 5:1–6 NASB).

This is a clear condemnation of those who unfairly profit from the labor of others—gathering wealth from the unpaid sweat of others. Woe indeed!

Conclusion

The coffee or tea we drink every morning, the chocolate we savor in the afternoons, and the countless other goods we consume on a daily basis are often so affordable because those who produce them are not paid appropriate wages, forcing them to live in poverty. Fair Trade therefore becomes an important issue for Christians because Scripture commands us in no uncertain terms to care for the poor, a mandate that becomes even more pressing for Christians in the United States because our wealth far exceeds that of the majority world. We suggest that Fair Trade provides Christians with an opportunity (even if it is a small one) to fulfill this biblical mandate. Certainly, Fair Trade comes with its own set of problems that limits its effectiveness in alleviating poverty, and even if it were perfect, it is not feasible to purchase everything from a Fair Trade market. Nevertheless, the realities of today's global economy should give Christian consumers pause when faced with our buying decisions. Has the item we are purchasing helped or hurt the poor, and with our purchase are we contributing to the problem? No matter how insignificant it may seem, making the decision to spend a few more dollars on our coffee and tea *does* make a difference.

3

Immigration

Whom Would Jesus Let in?

Matthew Soerens

Introduction

MANY CHRISTIANS FIND THEMSELVES conflicted when they consider how their faith might inform their response to issues of immigration within the United States, especially when it comes to the question of how to respond to immigrants who are present unlawfully. Scripture makes clear that Christians are to be subject to civil authorities, but also calls us repeatedly to welcome, love, and ensure the just treatment of immigrants. Ought we to love the immigrant who is present in violation of law, and, if so, what does that love look like both in terms of our individual interactions with undocumented immigrants and in terms of the public policies that we advocate?

The People behind the Public Policy Question

Like any public policy issue, immigration policy ultimately is important because it affects people—human beings made in the image of God (Gen 1:27), for whom Christ died (1 John 2:2). Many evangelical Christians view immigration first and foremost as a personal issue: how do I treat the immigrant who moves into my neighborhood, who shows up in my church, or who works at the restaurant where I go for lunch?

In some ways, the interpersonal questions (should I be kind or unkind to my immigrant neighbor? should the church welcome in the undocumented immigrant who wants help, or to be baptized and discipled, or to be equipped to disciple others?) are easier for most Christians to answer than the public policy question: who should the United States allow into our country, and how should we respond to those who have come in (or overstayed) unlawfully? The policy question is integral, though, because too many American evangelicals have allowed a political narrative about immigration—that immigrants are a threat—to blind them from a biblical perspective that would call them to see immigration as a missional opportunity. Unless we address the policy question from a distinctly biblical perspective, many will continue to miss the mission on our doorsteps.

Missiologists have found that immigrants are often amongst the most receptive groups of people to the gospel; all around the world, God is at work through the movement of people to advance his kingdom.[1] Scripture tells us that God has a design in the movement of people: that "from one man he made every nation of men, that they should inhabit the whole earth; and he determined the times set for them and the exact places where they should live" (Acts 17:26 NIV). While there are important economic and geopolitical reasons for why migration occurs, above them all is the hand of God in the movement of people for a particular purpose: "so that men would seek him and perhaps reach out for him and find him" (Acts 17:27 NIV 1984).

Missiologists have noted at least three ways that God is working through migration: through ministry *to* immigrants who do not yet know Jesus, *through* immigrants who function as agents of mission, ministering to their own people group, and *beyond* the immigrant experience, as immigrants—many of whom bring a vibrant Christian faith with them to their new country—share the gospel with native-born citizens of their host country who are not yet followers of Christ.[2] While many in American society see immigration as a threat, missiologist Tim Tennent argues that "the immigrant population actually presents the greatest hope for Christian renewal in North America."[3]

1. See Wan, *Diaspora Missiology*.
2. Lausanne, *Scattered to Gather*, 27–30.
3. Tennent, "Christian Perspective on Immigration."

Sadly, most American evangelicals are missing this missional opportunity. The Faith Communities Today survey finds that just one in ten evangelical churches in the U.S. has *any* sort of ministry or ministry partnership focused on reaching immigrants,[4] and even in those churches that do specifically seek to minister to immigrants, usually only a small fraction of the congregation is engaged.

I believe that the relative slowness to embrace this missional opportunity is a symptom of the fact that most American evangelicals do not think about immigration *as Christians*. A 2010 Pew Research Center poll found that just 12 percent of white evangelicals say their opinions about immigration are influenced primarily by their faith.[5] The vast majority view immigration through a different lens: based on the rhetoric of their favorite cable news personality, the position of their preferred political party, or their perceptions (often inaccurate) of the effects of immigration on their economic well-being. Consequently, polls find that most white evangelicals see immigrants as "a burden on our country" and believe that further immigration "threatens traditional American customs and values,"[6] and thus miss out on the missional opportunity.

Addressing the policy question from a distinctly Christian perspective, then, is vital both because it is a necessary element of seeking the justice that God requires (Isa 1:17) and because the policy question becomes a stumbling block that keeps many American evangelicals from responding in biblically faithful ways to the missional opportunity presented by immigration. We'll first look at what Scripture says that should inform our thinking of immigration, then consider how those principles might apply to American immigration policy.

The Bible and Immigration

A colleague of mine recently commented that, in more than sixty years of church-going, she had never heard a sermon about immigration. She's not alone: 84 percent of white evangelicals in the U.S. say they have never heard their pastor or other clergy discuss the topic of immigration.[7] That's not because the Scriptures are silent on the matter, though: immigration

4. Hartford Institute for Religion Research, "Faith Communities Today," 3.

5. Pew Research Center, "Few Say Religion Shapes," table 5.

6. Cited by Grant, "SBC Vote Reveals," para. 9.

7. Pew Research Center, "Few Say Religion Shapes," table 5.

is actually a common theme throughout the Bible. The Hebrew word *ger*—which most English translations render as "foreigner," "alien," or "sojourner," but which Tim Keller argues convincingly should actually be "immigrant"[8]—appears ninety-two times in the Old Testament.[9] By the count of theologian Orlando Espin, "Welcoming the stranger. . . is the most often repeated commandment in the Hebrew Scriptures, with the exception of the imperative to worship only the one God."[10]

The references to the immigrant in the Old Testament follow a few recurring themes. First, many of the heroes of the narrative of Scripture—Abraham, Jacob, Joseph, Ruth, David, Daniel—were themselves immigrants, crossing borders under many of the same circumstances as today's migrants: fleeing poverty and famine, aiming to reunify a family, seeking asylum, or trafficked involuntarily. The parallels between the biblical narrative and the realities of today's immigrants are many.

God also has a great deal to say about how to treat immigrants: he repeatedly challenges his people, the Israelites, to remember their own history as immigrants in the land of Egypt, and, once God has established them in the Promised Land, to allow their ancestors' experience to inform the way they treat the immigrants who come into the Promised Land. "Do not oppress a foreigner," God commands, "you yourselves know how it feels to be foreigners, because you were foreigners in Egypt" (Exod 23:9 NIV).

The immigrant appears frequently in the Old Testament alongside three other vulnerable groups of people who compose what Nicholas Wolterstorff calls the "quartet of the vulnerable": the resident alien, the orphan, the widow, and the impoverished.[11] God makes clear that he loves these vulnerable individuals, whom he commands his people to love and protect. "Do not oppress the widow or the fatherless, the foreigner or the poor" (Zech 7:10 NIV). The prophet Malachi warns that "those who defraud laborers of their wages, who oppress the widows and the fatherless, and deprive the foreigners among you of justice" will be judged alongside adulterers, perjurers, and sorcerers (Mal 3:5). "The Lord watches over the foreigner and sustains the fatherless and the widow," the psalmist proclaims, "but he frustrates the way of the wicked" (Ps 146:9 NIV).

8. Keller, *Generous Justice*, 193.

9. Soerens and Hwang, *Welcoming the Stranger*, 83.

10. Espin, "Immigration and Theology," 46–47.

11. Wolsterstorff, *Justice*, 76.

God not only loves immigrants, he also establishes specific rules to ensure that they could meet their basic needs, commanding the Israelites not to harvest the entirety of their fields, but to leave the edges "for the poor and for the foreigner residing among you" (Lev 23:22 NIV). God insists that the immigrant be granted the same labor protections as Israelites, including a Sabbath day's rest (Exod 20:10), freedom from oppression (Deut 24:14), and timely payment of wages (Deut 24:15). In almost every aspect of Israelite life, the immigrant was to "be treated as your native-born" (Lev 19:34 NIV), which stood in stark contrast to the laws of the societies surrounding Israel, which showed little regard for immigrants.[12]

In the New Testament, Jesus reiterates the command to love one's neighbor. His parable of the Good Samaritan—to the Jewish listener, someone of a different ethnic group and religious tradition—makes clear that the "neighbor" is defined broadly. The New Testament also repeatedly calls the Christian (Rom 12:13, 1 Pet 4:9), and church leaders in particular (1 Tim 5:10), to hospitality. To most contemporary readers, as Christine Pohl notes, hospitality "now chiefly refers to the entertainment of one's acquaintances at home and to the hospitality industry's provision of service through hotels and restaurants,"[13] but the hospitality to which Scripture calls us—*philoxenia*, in Greek—means "the love of strangers."[14] When we welcome a stranger, Scripture suggests that we might be welcoming "angels without knowing it" (Heb 13:2 NIV) or even, as the Parable of the Sheep and the Goats has it, Christ himself (Matt 25:35, 40).

Submitting to the Governing Authorities (or "What Part of Illegal Don't You Understand?")

The Bible has much to say that would guide how a Christian thinks about immigration—the preceding is just a cursory, incomprehensive summary—but it does not give any explicit instructions about how to respond to *illegal immigration*. Of course, most immigrants in the United States—about 70 percent according to the U.S. Department of Homeland Security—are present lawfully, either as naturalized U.S. citizens, lawful permanent residents, or valid temporary visa-holders.[15] With about 30 percent of the

---

12. Carroll R., *Christians at the Border*, 102.

13. Pohl, *Making Room*, 36.

14. Nathan, "Hospitality," 11.

15. Hoefer, Rytina, and Baker, "Estimates of the Unauthorized Immigrant Population," 4.

foreign-born population present unlawfully, though, the question of how to respond to the undocumented is too significant to ignore.

Scripture does speak to the question of how the Christ-follower should relate to the civil government: Rom 13 insists that everyone ought to "be subject to the governing authorities, for there is no authority except that which God has established. The authorities that exist have been established by God" (Rom 13:1 NIV). Paul goes on to say that "whoever rebels against the authority is rebelling against what God has instituted, and those who do so will bring judgment on themselves" because "rulers do not bear the sword for no reason" (Rom 13:2, 4 NIV). Peter similarly admonishes followers of Jesus to "submit yourselves for the Lord's sake to every human authority" (1 Pet 2:13 NIV). We are clearly and repeatedly called to love and defend the cause of the immigrant, but also to be subject to the laws of the state. How, then, do we respond to immigrants whose very presence is a violation of law?

Fortunately, these commands do not really contradict one another, at least for most American Christians, because there are actually very few ways that a U.S. citizen could run afoul of U.S. immigration law. Federal law does not prohibit any of the activities that most churches or individuals might take part in as they relate to undocumented immigrants: we can preach the gospel to undocumented immigrants, teach them in Sunday School (or let them teach us), provide food assistance from a food pantry, and offer English classes—and never violate the law. There is no legal requirement on normal citizens or churches to report those whom they suspect are present unlawfully. The only likely area where a church or individual could violate the law would be by employing an immigrant who is not authorized to work. In general, we can minister effectively and still comply with the law.

It is important to note, though, that some states have passed laws that could change this dynamic. Most notably, states such as Arizona and Alabama have made it a crime—punishable by up to ten years in some cases—to knowingly transport someone who is undocumented "in furtherance of the unlawful presence of the alien."[16] Courts have yet to conclusively decide whether driving someone to church, to English classes, or to the hospital would qualify, but the fact that certain individuals (law enforcement, first responders, and child protective services) are exempted, but not church staff or volunteers, has many concerned with what they view as an infringement on their religious liberty. After all, bringing people—regardless

16. State of Alabama, "H.B. 56," 34.

of their legal status—to church is a primary strategy for evangelism for many churches, which in turn is central to their mission, and transporting someone in need to get help is precisely the example that Jesus gives of what it means to fulfill the Great Commandment's injunction to "love your neighbor as yourself" (Luke 10:27 NIV). As pastor Rick Warren notes, "A good Samaritan doesn't stop and ask the injured person. 'Are you legal or illegal?'"[17]

These new laws at the state level—and the possibility that similar legislation could become law at the federal level, such as a vaguely-worded, narrowly-failed 2005 bill that would have made it a felony offense to "assist" someone undocumented to reside in the United States[18]—force an important question: are there ever instances when the Christian, in order to follow biblical commands, must disobey the law of the state?

Almost all Christian traditions acknowledge that, in certain circumstances, civil disobedience is permissible and even required. Martin Luther King, Jr. was echoing St. Augustine when he argued that "an unjust law is no law at all."[19] While disobeying the unjust segregation laws of the Jim Crow-era American South, King and other Civil Rights leaders remained "subject" to them, non-violently accepting imprisonment and other consequences, however unjust, to their disobedience. They followed in the biblical tradition of heroes like the Hebrew midwives who defied Pharaoh's genocidal order (Exod 1:17), Shadrach, Meshach, and Abednego who refused to worship Nebuchadnezzar's idol and went to the fiery furnace (Dan 3:18–19), and the Apostle Peter, who boldly told the authorities who had commanded the apostles to stop preaching in the name of Jesus, "We must obey God rather than human beings!" (Acts 5:29 NIV).

Whether or not laws such as Arizona's sufficiently infringe upon religious freedom that civil disobedience is warranted for (or even required of) the Christian is perhaps a question of individual conscience, but I believe that Christians should use their voice in a democratic government to fervently oppose any legislation that could limit our rights to minister lawfully in the first place.

The question of Scripture's repeated commands to be subject to civil government's authority is even more challenging for believers who are undocumented immigrants. Not long ago, I discussed this with a friend—a

---

17. Qtd. in Grossman, "Rick Warren Speaks Up," para. 14.

18. American Immigration Lawyers Association, "The Border Protection," 5.

19. Martin Luther King, "Letter from a Birmingham Jail," 89.

theologically-educated Baptist—who is anguished by his unlawful presence in the United States. He came to the U.S. about twenty years ago from Mexico, desperate to provide for his wife and two children. He wants desperately to get right with the law, but he has found that current law provides no hope of legalizing his status, even if he were to return to Mexico. His challenge is that he also takes very seriously the biblical teaching that "anyone who does not provide for their relatives, and especially for their own household, has denied the faith and is worse than an unbeliever" (1 Tim 5:8 NIV). In his case, he does not believe he could provide for his family—now three people more than when he left his village, where the economic situation has not substantially improved—if he returned.

I am not sure what the right, biblical answer is to my friend's dilemma. I am quite certain, though, that a legal framework that forces individuals to choose between obeying the law and providing for their families could be improved. I—and many pastors of immigrant congregations around the country—would love to be able to advise people in this situation to do both: to get right with the government (paying a fine for their violation of law as necessary) *and* to stay and provide for their families, but that would require reform of current U.S. immigration law.

Public Policy Responses

What might such a reform look like? Most evangelical leaders are actually remarkably unified both in recognizing the need for reform and the basic principles that should guide it. More than 150 prominent evangelical leaders have signed onto a statement calling for immigration reform that:

- *Respects* the God-given dignity of every person.
- *Protects* the unity of the immediate family.
- *Respects* the rule of law.
- *Guarantees* secure national borders.
- *Ensures* fairness to taxpayers.
- *Establishes* a path toward legal status and/or citizenship for those who qualify and who wish to become permanent residents.[20]

The diverse set of leaders who have affirmed these basic principles stretches across denominations, ethnicities, political affiliation, and

20. Evangelical Immigration Table, "Evangelical Statement," para. 2.

geography, including many of the most influential Christian leaders in the country. Signatories include popular authors such as Max Lucado, Eric Metaxas, Shane Claiborne, and Margaret Feinberg; presidents and other academic leaders from some of the most respected evangelical seminaries and colleges; leaders of parachurch organizations including Focus on the Family, World Vision, InterVarsity Christian Fellowship, the Navigators, World Relief, and Prison Fellowship; influential pastors such as Bill Hybels, J.D. Greear, and Rich Nathan; and executives of eighteen evangelical denominations, including the Southern Baptist Convention, the Assemblies of God, the Evangelical Free Church of America, the Christian & Missionary Alliance, and the Church of the Nazarene.

What might those principles look like when translated into actual policy? Not all of those named above necessarily agree on the specifics of legislation, but what many have advocated is a Comprehensive Immigration Reform policy that would essentially have three fundamental goals:

1. Make it *harder* to immigrate or work unlawfully.

2. Make it *easier* to immigrate lawfully.

3. Require and allow those who are currently undocumented to pay a fine to get right with the law, then give them the opportunity to earn the right to stay permanently and fully integrate into the United States.

Let me explain each of those three elements in context:

Make It Harder to Immigrate or Work Unlawfully

No one thinks that illegal immigration is a good thing. It is both a potential problem for our national security as well as a mockery of the biblical ideal of the rule of law for our immigration laws to be routinely ignored. We should do everything reasonably possible to ensure that everyone who enters the United States does so with a valid visa. Since about 45 percent of the undocumented immigrants in the U.S. did not enter illegally in the first place, but overstayed a valid temporary visa, we also need better systems to ensure that visitors respect the terms of their visa.[21] One of the easiest ways to deter both unlawful entries as well as visa over-stayers would be to develop a reasonable, enforceable workplace authorization system: almost all undocumented immigrants, regardless of their mode of entry, come to

21. Pew Hispanic Center, "Modes of Entry," 1.

work, and if they were unable to find work without the proper documents, they would be unlikely to come.

It's important to note that this is actually the one element (of the three elements of Comprehensive Immigration Reform presented here) on which the U.S. government has made substantial progress in the last several years, beginning under the Bush Administration and continuing under the Obama Administration. The U.S.-Mexico border is more secure than at any time since the 1970s.[22] Because of the confluence of an exponential increase in border-security spending over the last decade and the dramatic slowdown in attempted unlawful border crossings (primarily a result of the lack of available jobs in the midst of an economic slowdown), the U.S. government now spends about $7,500 *per person* apprehended attempting to enter unlawfully, up from $1,400 just five years earlier.[23] With net migration between Mexico and the United States now at zero,[24] some border patrol agents actually say they are "bored."[25] Though politicians sensationalize isolated cases of violence along the border, crime data shows that violent crime rates in the border region have been on the decline for the past several years and are actually lower than both the national average and the crime rates in other parts of border states.[26]

Much of the progress in securing our borders, though, is probably due to the economic downturn. If and when the U.S. economy continues to grow rapidly, more jobs will be created, including many jobs in sectors (such as agriculture) that few American workers have proven willing to perform at prevailing wages, and, without reform, illegal immigration will resume.[27] In the past, the federal government has often turned a blind eye to unauthorized work with easily-falsifiable documents. That's at least in part because unauthorized immigrant labor plays a vital economic role—contrary to popular perception, more than 95 percent of economists surveyed by the *Wall Street Journal* say illegal immigrants have benefited the U.S. economy[28]—and if employment authorization laws were strictly

22. Miroff and Booth, "Arrests of Illegal Immigrants," para. 1.

23. National Immigration Forum, "Immigration Enforcement," 1.

24. Passel, Cohn, and Gonzalez-Barrera, "Net Migration from Mexico," 6.

25. Marosi, "Plunge in Border Crossings," para. 8.

26. Gomez, Gillum, and Johnson, "U.S. Border Cities," para. 6.

27. American Farm Bureau Federation, "Impact of Migrant Farm Labor Restrictions," 1.

28. Annet, "Illegal Immigrants and the Economy," para. 8.

enforced and borders carefully guarded without amending our current visa system, our national economy would suffer. Since no president wants to preside over an economic downtown, administrations of both major political parties have, for the past several decades, regularly turned a blind eye to unauthorized work, even while undocumented immigrants, 75 percent of whom the Social Security Administration estimates have payroll taxes deducted from their paychecks,[29] contribute as much as $12 billion a year to the Social Security system, a fund from which, without legal status, they will never be eligible to benefit.[30]

The wink-and-nod system employed for the past several decades mocks the biblical principle of rule of law (Rom 13:1) as both immigrants and employers violate the law, usually without penalty. It also opens up vulnerable undocumented immigrants to exploitation, since their lack of legal status makes many afraid to report unsafe working conditions, wage theft, or even situations of human trafficking, where they are forced or coerced to work involuntarily.[31] The only alternative, though, if we want a growing economy *as well as* a genuinely secure border and consistently-enforced employment authorization laws, is to enact the second element of Comprehensive Immigration Reform, which is . . .

Make It Easier to Immigrate Lawfully

Most Americans, who never have any reason to interact with our federal immigration legal system, presume that the United States of America has some sort of a logical, functional legal system; I certainly did until just a few years ago. I presumed that there was some process by which someone who wanted to immigrate to the United States to fill an available job for which no U.S. citizen was applying could fill out some paperwork and enter in a lawful fashion. I supposed that, like a visit to the Department of Motor Vehicles or some other government agency, it was a bureaucratic process with lots of paperwork and fees and probably not the best customer service, but that if someone were to fill out the right form and wait a reasonable period, they could migrate to the U.S. Those who entered illegally or overstayed a visa, I supposed, were merely too impatient to wait their turn in line, or perhaps too uneducated to wade through the bureaucracy.

29. Porter, "Illegal Immigrants Are Bolstering," para. 15.
30. Schumacher-Matos, "How Illegal Immigrants Are Helping," para. 3.
31. Polaris Project, "Labor Trafficking," para. 10.

The reality, which I learned when I began working for a Christian ministry called World Relief in a legal counselor role, is that our current immigration laws, though they work for some, are an archaic mess of quotas that are woefully out of touch with—and unresponsive to—a dynamic U.S. labor market.

Under current law—much of which was written back in 1965—there are four primary ways that a would-be immigrant could come to and work in the U.S. on a permanent basis: through a family sponsor, through an employer sponsor, by winning the Diversity Lottery, or if designated as a refugee fleeing persecution.

Our family-based immigration system, which accounts for at least 226,000 permanent visas per year, allows U.S. citizens and Lawful Permanent Residents (those with "green cards") to file petitions for their close relatives (but not for grandparents, cousins, uncles and aunts, or other more distant relatives).[32] The system works fairly well if you happen to be the spouse, minor child, or parent of an adult U.S. citizen (and presuming that the beneficiary has not already entered the United States unlawfully), but the system is very backlogged for most other qualifying relationships as a result of quotas written into the law. A pastor near me, for example, migrated lawfully and filed for his wife and minor children back in El Salvador as soon as he arrived in the U.S. with his green card; he had to wait about five years before they were able to migrate to join him. The worst-case scenario is for a U.S. citizen who files a petition for her sibling in the Philippines: those cases are currently being processed only if they were filed prior to 1989, a backlog of more than two decades.[33]

The employment-based immigration system is, in my analysis, even more problematic. There were 140,000 employer-sponsored immigrant visas available in 2011.[34] The vast majority of these visas—all but 5,000— can only possibly be granted to "highly-skilled" workers, defined by law as those with advanced degrees or exceptional abilities.[35] The U.S. labor market, though, requires many more foreign-born workers than that limited quota each year in sectors that do not require a Master's degree. To put that number in historical perspective, a century ago, 5,000 immigrants came through Ellis Island on an average day, most of whom, if we had the same

32. Soerens and Hwang, *Welcoming the Stranger*, 72–73.

33. U.S. State Department, "Visa Bulletin," 2.

34. Monger and Yankay, "U.S. Legal Permanent Residents," 6.

35. Paral, "No Way In," para. 10.

classifications and restrictions then as we do now, would have been deemed "low-skilled."[36]

The third possibility for lawful immigration is to win the Diversity Visa Lottery. The Diversity Lottery provides for 50,000 immigrant visas per year to individuals who have at least a high school education or two years of professional experience in particular fields. The odds of winning the lottery were only about one in 250 for Fiscal Year 2013.[37] Furthermore, certain countries, including Mexico, the Philippines, India, China, South Korea, and other countries that already send many emigrants to the U.S., are ineligible even to apply.

The final way that an individual might be eligible to immigrate lawfully to the U.S. is if he meets the legal definition of a refugee, an individual who has fled his country because of persecution on account of his race, religion, political opinion, national origin, or social group.[38] In Fiscal Year 2011, the U.S. admitted about 56,000 refugees; approximately 25,000 more individuals were granted asylum, meaning that they were found once already in the United States to meet the legal definition of a refugee.[39] Providing safe haven to those fleeing persecution—including many who are targeted specifically because of their Christian faith—is a vital humanitarian function of our immigration system as well as an important foreign policy tool. It is important to understand, though, that those fleeing poverty or natural disasters do not legally qualify as refugees. And even among those who do meet the legal definition of a refugee—the United Nations High Commissioner for Refugees counts 15.4 million refugees worldwide (not including Internally Displaced People)[40]—only a fraction of one percent each year will be resettled to the U.S., so the fact that a person who is forced to flee persecution in their country is certainly not a "golden ticket" to be allowed to migrate to the U.S.

This system works fairly well for some individuals, but it leaves a lot of would-be immigrants without an option. We often hear that immigrants without legal status should "go home and come back the legal way," but the

36. Statue of Liberty-Ellis Island Foundation, "Ellis Island Approaches Centennial," para. 1.

37. U.S. Department of State, "Diversity Visa Program," 24.

38. Soerens and Hwang, *Welcoming the Stranger*, 78.

39. Martin and Yankay, "Refugees and Asylees," 4, 6.

40. United Nations High Commissioner for Refugees, "UNHCR Global Trends 2010," 3.

reality for many is that there was probably no legal possibility of coming in the first place, and no legal way of returning if they were to leave now. A friend of mine who migrated unlawfully in 1990 is quite typical: her only family members in the U.S. with legal status were cousins who were ineligible to petition for her; she came to work, but the fast food restaurant jobs she has held for more than two decades would not qualify her as "highly-skilled," so her odds of an employment-based visa were practically zero; she is from Mexico and thus ineligible to apply for the Diversity Visa Lottery; and, though she was fleeing poverty, she was not fleeing persecution. For someone in her situation, there is no line to wait in to migrate lawfully: it would not matter if she waited twenty years or two hundred years, she would probably never have been eligible to migrate lawfully to the U.S.

The problem is that, since there were jobs available and employment authorization laws were ignored, she came anyway and quickly found work. Now she is fairly well integrated into U.S. society, with two U.S. citizen children whose first language is English, and her employer does not want to lose her. Our society, which appreciates cheap fast food, does not want to lose her, either.

If we are to be serious about securing the border and enforcing employment authorization laws, we need to adjust our dysfunctional visa system. That does not mean opening the doors wide open, but it does mean setting our visa quotas at levels that meet the needs of and are sensitive to the U.S. labor market, rather than our current static quota, which might have made sense in 1965 but does not today. In keeping with our national values, we should also adjust the family reunification visas so that a wife need not wait years to be reunited to her husband and minor children, and we should continue—and consider expanding—our efforts to provide refuge to those fleeing persecution.

This sort of visa reform should be common sense, especially for those who believe the free market—with minimized restrictions on the flow of goods and capital as well as labor—is the most efficient economic system. A combination of a reformed visa system, border security, and an enforceable employment authorization system should dramatically reduce future illegal immigration while also allowing our economy to grow. The most controversial question, though, remains: how do we respond to those who are already present unlawfully?

Require and Allow Those Who Are Currently Undocumented to Pay a Fine to Get Right with the Law, Then Give Them the Opportunity to Earn the Right to Stay Permanently and Fully Integrate into the United States

There are really only a few possible options for what to do with the estimated 11.5 million immigrants currently living in the United States without legal status.[41] On one extreme, the federal government could attempt to deport all of them. There are a few reasons why almost no one in Congress, on either side of the political aisle, has realistically suggested this proposal. First of all, the cost to the U.S. government to undergo such a massive deportation effort would be huge: the Department of Homeland Security estimates that the cost would be about eighty billion dollars;[42] some independent estimates peg the cost at $285 billion.[43] Those are just the costs of *removing* 11.5 million people, not including the costs of trying to keep them from coming back, which many—separated from U.S. citizen spouses or children—are likely to attempt. Furthermore, the cost to the U.S. gross domestic product of not having those undocumented immigrants participating in the economy as workers, consumers, and taxpayers could be as much, according to one study, as $2.6 *trillion* over a decade.[44]

On the opposite end of the spectrum, there are some who believe the solution is to grant amnesty to all those who are undocumented. I do not believe that amnesty is the best policy, but I find a bit ironic the derision with which many—including some Christians—speak of amnesty. After all, amnesty is merely a synonym for grace, which is at the very center of the gospel. Scripture makes clear that I am saved from my sins by Christ's atoning death on the cross, "not by works" (Eph 2:9). I have Christian friends who do advocate amnesty for undocumented immigrants—a forgiving and forgetting of the offense of those who have entered the U.S. or have overstayed a visa unlawfully—who point to Jesus's parable of the unmerciful servant (Matt 18:21–35) as a rationale. We who have been forgiven so much (by God), they argue, should be quick to forgive others.

41. Hoefer, Rytina, and Baker, "Estimates of the Unauthorized Immigrant Population," 3.

42. Bennett, "Senators Ask About Cost," para. 12.

43. Kasperkevic, Jana. "Deporting All of America's Illegal Immigrants," para. 4.

44. Hinojosa-Ojeda, Raul, "The Economic Benefits," 177.

While I agree that there is a place for mercy in our treatment of un-documented immigrants, there is an important distinction between Jesus's command to his disciples to forgive extravagantly (Matt 18:22) and the role of the state, which Scripture says is God's instrument "to bring punishment" (Rom 13:4 NIV). As an individual, I'm called to forgive over and over again, but if the state were to forgive every offense, there could be no order.

The question, then, is not whether the state should forgive (or, as we do now, ignore) violations of law, but rather what an appropriate penalty would be. Unlawful presence in the United States is a civil (not criminal) offense,[45] and, while clearly unlawful, it does not require malicious intent; in fact, while we may not condone the breaking of law, I suspect that most Americans would consider crossing a border or overstaying a visa if it were the only option available to provide for their families. With the exception of the relatively few who have committed serious crimes, then, an appropriate penalty could be a reasonable monetary fine, from which those who were brought into the country as children or trafficked in under force, fraud, or coercion should be exempt. (Those that have committed serious criminal offenses *would* be deported.)

Having paid a fine, these individuals could then be granted a proba-tionary legal status permitting them to work and travel lawfully. After a few years, having demonstrated that they have been paying taxes, working to-ward learning English, and avoiding criminal problems (all of which most undocumented immigrants are already doing), they would be eligible for Lawful Permanent Resident status. Five years later, like any other Lawful Permanent Resident, they would be eligible to apply for naturalization if they can pass a test of spoken and written English, American history, and government (a test that surveys suggest at least a third of Americans would probably fail).[46] "Such a solution," says theologian John Piper, "would give honor to the law and show mercy to the immigrants."[47]

This sort of Comprehensive Immigration Reform is actually remark-ably popular. 72 percent of Americans—including a majority of both Republicans and Democrats—favor such a plan, which includes both border security and a path to citizenship for undocumented immigrants.[48]

---

45. Donohue, "Christie Clarifies," para. 3.

46. Ho, "Survey," para. 3.

47. Piper, "What Should We Do About Illegal Immigration?," para. 4.

48. Pew Research Center, "Beyond Red vs. Blue," 81.

Sixty-five percent of white evangelicals surveyed agreed.[49] Yet when such legislation was last considered in Congress—pushed forward by Republican President George W. Bush—it failed to pass through the Senate, with most of the opposition coming from the President's own party.[50]

The reason that a largely popular reform would fail is that a vocal minority opposed to the bill—who characterized it, despite a proposed fine for each undocumented immigrant of $5,000,[51] as "amnesty"—flooded congressional offices with phone calls, faxes, and letters. The majority of Americans who supported the bill, however, were largely silent. After all, the individuals most dramatically impacted by the bill, immigrants themselves, could not vote, and polls suggest that immigration policy ranks near the bottom of issues that concern American voters most.[52] It's not *our* problem.

Conclusion

It *is* our problem, though. The church, as William Temple once said, "exists for the benefit of its non-members."[53] If the Church will not speak out for the interests of those who are marginalized in our society, who will? If we have a biblical ecclesiology, we also recognize that, in the words of National Association of Evangelicals president Leith Anderson, "they are us,"[54] because immigrants account for the fastest growth in American evangelicalism.[55] Scripture teaches that their suffering is to be our suffering as well, since we are all part of one, interdependent body (1 Cor 12:26). That's one reason that it is so important that American evangelicals recognize that, as good stewards of our citizenship, we are called to "speak up for those who [at least on a political level] cannot speak for themselves" (Prov 31:8 NIV), advocating for policies that are consistent with biblical values of justice, compassion, and hospitality.

Of course, advocacy is just one of many ways that the church should respond to immigration. We can minister directly to the needs of immigrants,

49. Qtd. in Grant, "SBC Vote Reveals," para. 12.

50. Pear and Hulse, "Immigration Bill Fails," para. 4.

51. Dell'orto, "Costs Worry Immigration Advocates," para. 1.

52. NBC News/Wall Street Journal, "Study 12768," 13.

53. Qtd. in Yancey, *Grace Notes,* 87.

54. Anderson, "Evangelicals for Immigration Reform," para. 6.

55. Johnson, "USA Evangelicals/Evangelicals in Global Context," para. 6.

providing English classes, counseling, youth programs, and (with proper training and accreditation) legal services. We can offer the simple gift of friendship. We can share the hope of the gospel—while recognizing that immigrants can be agents, as well as objects, of mission.[56]

The question of how we engage immigration policy, though, is vital to the efficacy of our efforts to respond to the missional opportunity of immigration. We cannot effectively minister to undocumented immigrants while ignoring the injustices of immigration policy any more than one could minister to African-Americans in the Jim Crow-era American South while staying silent on the question of the Civil Rights Movement. Our presentation of the gospel—that Jesus loves and died for each person—rings hollow if our words, actions, or our support for particular political candidates tells our immigrant neighbors that, while Jesus may love them, we loathe them and would prefer they not be in our communities.

To the contrary, when we welcome immigrants and advocate with them for just, compassionate, and reasonable policies, we live the truth of the gospel that we proclaim: that Christ welcomes each of us in our imperfection. In the process, as many evangelical churches and denominations are already experiencing, we may also find that the immigrants arriving in our communities strengthen and revitalize American evangelicalism.

56. Martinez, "Latin American Theology."

4

Birth Control
When Is the Quiver Full?

William R. Osborne

Introduction

Few contemporary issues have garnered as much attention over the last fifty years in both the church and the public square as birth control. From the rise of the oral contraceptive pill in the 1960s to the watershed decision of *Roe v. Wade* on January 17th, 1973, birth control has continued to be the topic of numerous debates, conferences, elections, and legislation. Internationally, countries like China with its burgeoning population continue to come under public scrutiny over forced reproductive control in order to maintain its one child policy. Despite all of this global attention, the sheer vastness and complexity of the issue has left many in the evangelical world puzzling over how to move forward within the context of their own immediate families. Recent health care legislation within the United States has expanded the discussion beyond small-scale family decisions—birth control has risen to the point of national focus as some Christian organizations and employers question whether or not they can comply with federal healthcare mandates.

Provided both the importance and personal nature of the birth control debate, it is not surprising that large camps have formed on both ends of the spectrum. Many evangelical Christians comfortably locate themselves within the anti-abortion camp, yet the debate remains as to whether or not—and how—Christians should seek to "control" the number of children they have, or whether contraceptive methods of birth control are ethical at all. A small but influential movement within Christianity, the "Quiverfull" movement, frequently cites passages like Ps 127:4–5a (ESV) to argue biblically that any form of conception control (which some in the movement dub "planned barrenness") is unbiblical:

> Like arrows in the hand of a warrior
> are the children of one's youth.
> Blessed is the man
> who fills his quiver with them!

While it is not the majority position in evangelicalism at present, this movement has received much attention in books,[1] newspapers,[2] and even cable television shows such as TLC's 19 *Kids and Counting* and *Kate Plus 8*. Is every Christian family called by God to have as many children as possible? For those seeking to take the Bible seriously, the question then remains: When is the quiver full?

It is critical for Christians to understand the facts surrounding the discussion—both biblical and scientific—when making the decision about birth control. For this reason, we will first examine what the Bible has to say about having and not having children. Then, we will explore how Christians can walk in obedience to what the Bible says within the modern medical context in which we live, focusing specifically on hormonal forms of birth control such as "the pill," long-term implants, IUDs, and emergency contraception (Plan B). Unfortunately, this brief discussion cannot address every issue or individual case study that will arise regarding family planning, but if the modest goal of helping people think through birth control with a more biblical perspective is accomplished, this article will have succeeded in what it sets out to do.

1. Joyce, *Quiverfull*.
2. Zernike, "And Baby Makes How Many?"

Birth Control: What Does the Bible Say?

Having a Child Begins at Conception—Not Birth

Any serious discussion of birth control must address the question of when human life begins because therein lies the heart of the debate for many Christians. The Bible presents the Triune God of Christianity as the source of all living beings; therefore, his purposes extend to those beings from the moment life begins. However, the issue is more a question of when a person actually becomes *a person*. Both sperm and egg are "living" things, but at what point do they create a new, individual person who must be treated as such? John Jefferson Davis helpfully addresses this when he says: "A 'person' is a being to which God relates in a personal way; it is God's initiative in relationships that 'personalizes' the creature."[3] If personhood is achieved when God relates to us personally, then the Bible seems to indicate that this divinely initiated relationship begins at what scientists call conception, or syngamy (the creation of an individual zygote's genetic code through the combination of parental DNA).

Several biblical passages speak to our Creator-God's intimate relationship with the unborn. In Ps 139:13–16 (ESV) we read:

> For you formed my inward parts;
> you knitted me together in my mother's womb.
> I praise you, for I am fearfully and wonderfully made.
> Wonderful are your works;
> my soul knows it very well.
> My frame was not hidden from you,
> when I was being made in secret,
> intricately woven in the depths of the earth.
> Your eyes saw my unformed substance;
> in your book were written, every one of them,
> the days that were formed for me,
> when as yet there was none of them.

Jeremiah 1:5 (ESV) says:

> Before I formed you in the womb I knew you,
> and before you were born I consecrated you;
> I appointed you a prophet to the nations.

And finally, Paul says in Gal 1:15 (ESV)

---

3. Davis, *Evangelical Ethics*, 162.

> But when he had set me apart from before I was born [lit. "from my mother's womb"], and who called me by his grace, was pleased to reveal his Son to me, in order that I might preach him among the Gentiles, I did not immediately consult with anyone.

In Ps 139, David poetically declares that it was God who created him in his mother's womb. Even before he was born, God knew his tiny embryonic "frame," peering with divine eyes into the mysterious depths of his human "being" (see also Job 10:8–12). The Lord had even established the entire length of David's life while he was still an "unformed substance." There is a real temptation in Western society to divide reality into segments of time—that is, *reality* is now. However, David writes in Ps 139 that before any of his days had come into existence, the Lord had already charted out a "history" for him.

Similarly, Jer 1:5 and Gal 1:15 reveal the Lord's long-established plan for Jeremiah and Paul that began before either of them were born. In God's eternal plan he had ordained Jeremiah and Paul for their particular ministries. Lest we think that these two monumental figures are special cases, Eph 2:10 (ESV) states that the entire believing community is God's "workmanship, created in Christ Jesus for good works, which God prepared beforehand, that we should walk in them." The Bible speaks quite clearly to the fact that life and personhood for an individual begins before they are born.

Understanding the Bible's teaching that conception is the beginning of a child's life radically affects the birth control debate. It must be stated early on that, while not the "unpardonable sin," any form of birth control that leads to the death of a conceived baby in the mother's womb is unbiblical and immoral.

Having a Child Is a Blessing

Genesis 1:28 (ESV) says: "And God blessed them. And God said to them, 'Be fruitful and multiply and fill the earth and subdue it and have dominion over the fish of the sea and over the birds of the heavens and over every living thing that moves on the earth.'" A similar exhortation is found in Gen 9:7 with Noah and Gen 35:9–12 with Jacob. The words "be fruitful and multiply" in these passages have been interpreted by some in the "Quiverfull" movement as meaning God's blessing is also a mandate that applies universally to all married couples. It then follows that every married couple should recognize the procreative purpose of their one-flesh union and fulfill the command by practicing maximum fertility. While this interpretation rightly recognizes the importance of procreation within the divinely appointed institute of marriage, this divine exhortation should not be understood or applied as an individual command.

First, the birth of children in these passages serves to demonstrate God's blessing upon those he has chosen to bless. When the children of Israel sojourned in Egypt, God blessed them and they grew large in number (see Exod 1:7), and their God-given increase was proof of the Lord's hand upon them. Many times in the Old Testament God's blessing is summarized by numerical increase—whether it is children, livestock, land, or riches. Deuteronomy 28:2–5 (ESV) says:

> And all these blessings shall come upon you and overtake you, if you obey the voice of the Lord your God. Blessed shall you be in the city, and blessed shall you be in the field. Blessed shall be the fruit of your womb and the fruit of your ground and the fruit of your cattle, the increase of your herds and the young of your flock.

The people of Israel will experience this series of blessings, *if they obey the voice of Yahweh.* The blessing is not the command; it is the divinely promised *outcome* of heeding the command. The multiplication of children is listed alongside the increase of monetary blessings. This is largely because in the ancient world more children meant more workers, which in turn meant more productivity and consequently more money. This reality does not equate children with mere possessions, however, but indicates that the breadth of the Lord's blessing reaches all living things—be it people, animals, or plants. When Yahweh blesses, life is the result. Every child that has ever been born in this world, by their very birth, has demonstrated the creative power and blessing of God. The result is that "God does not command humans to be fruitful. Rather, he himself will bless his creatures and see to it that they are fruitful."[4]

Second, since the blessings in Gen 1:28 and Gen 9:7 are given to the human representatives Adam and Noah at key moments in the history of creation, this imperative to "be fruitful and multiply" is best understood as a general directive for all humanity and not as a requirement for every individual or every couple.[5] However, this does indicate that God has built into

---

4. Van Leeuwen, "Be Fruitful and Multiply," 60.

5. Grisanti, "Birth Control and the Christian," 91.

the very fabric of creation and the institution of marriage a deep theological value for procreation. We could say that within the context of a covenant relationship between a man and a woman, having sexual intercourse naturally produces children and God declares this to be very good in Gen 1:31. This divinely created relation between marriage and children should lead every married couple to consider seriously how their family can reflect this created order, whether through child bearing or adoption. In conclusion, I do not believe Gen 1:28 can serve as a proof-text for demanding every married couple to have children. However, given the portrayal of marriage and family in the first chapters of Genesis, I would be suspicious of any couple who wants to be married while doggedly opposing the idea of children.

Does Having a Child Mean Getting More Blessings?

> So, if the Bible affirms that children are good gifts from God, are couples missing out on God's blessings by not having children, or even by limiting the number? If God demonstrated his blessing upon humanity and later his covenant people Israel by multiplying their children, does that mean the more children you have the more blessings you have? Mary Pride, in her highly influential book *The Way Home: Beyond Feminism, Back to Reality* says: The two methods Christians use to plan their families—(1) spacing and (2) limiting family size—both have one thing in common: *they make a cutoff point on how many blessings a family is willing to accept.* Can anyone find one single Bible verse that says Christians should refuse God's blessings?[6]

Arguments that make claims such as: "Children are a blessing, therefore we should all have as many as possible because all blessings are good" are built upon biblical half-truths. As seen above, the Bible celebrates the blessing of children, but it does not follow that people are therefore required to have as many children as possible in order to be blessed. One of the most frequently mentioned verses in this discussion is Ps 127:3–5 (ESV):

> Behold, children are a heritage from the lord,
> the fruit of the womb a reward.
> Like arrows in the hand of a warrior
> are the children of one's youth.
> Blessed is the man

6. Pride, *The Way Home*, 76.

who fills his quiver with them!
He shall not be put to shame
when he speaks with his enemies in the gate.

This familiar psalm begins with builders and watchmen laboring in vain un-less the Lord's sovereign hand is at work in their tasks. Verse 2 addresses the vanity of hard work and anxiety over life's necessities, for the Lord "gives to his beloved sleep." Daniel Estes has rightly recognized the wisdom themes of vanity and toil in the early verses of Ps 127 and notes that they give an initial picture of human striving apart from Yahweh.[7] With this picture of vain human effort to build, defend, and provide in view, verse 3 presents the reassuring reality that Yahweh's blessing through the giving of children continues. Children are compared to arrows—an offensive, long-distance weapon in the ancient world—and "blessed is the man who fills his quiver with them!" We might summarize the progression of the psalm in this way: Apart from the Lord, the world is characterized by futile toil and hard work that leaves a person wondering whether or not life is but a fading horizon before the grave. But by producing and rearing godly children, hope can be found in that people can extend their legacy and significance beyond their days—and this hope is a blessing. This wisdom-filled psalm records an ongoing general truth. Children do provide a sense of hope in the face of death. Many grandparents can testify to the vitality and happiness small ones can bring when running through the house to give hugs. However, this verse does not indicate that the number of children conceived is pro-portionate or in any way equal to the amount of blessing a family receives from the Lord.

In essence, blessings are intended to drive us back to the Giver, not the gifts themselves. The goal of the Christian life is not to get more blessings, but to get more of God. And as helpful as Pride's book is at addressing many of the cultural shifts that have given way to a culture of abortion, her argument on this particular issue fails to take into account a full biblical understanding of blessing that moves from an Old Testament perspective to a New Testament perspective.

The biblical story begins with God creating the world and blessing humanity that they might fill it and rule as his representatives on earth. He gave Abraham a three-part promise that included blessing, land, and offspring, and this promise serves as the launching point for the remain-der of the Old Testament. The promise of offspring in the book of Genesis

---

7. Estes, "Like Arrows in the Hand of a Warrior," 304–11.

overcomes threat after threat in the early history of Israel. Both Sarah and Rebekah have children despite their previous barrenness. Recalling the Deuteronomy passage above, God's promise of blessing remained after the Exodus and took the form of multiplication of children, livestock, crops, and years in the Land of Promise. However, we must ask the question: How does this concept of blessings transfer into the New Covenant community?

Many discussions about the blessing of children err in not transposing their understanding of divine blessings from an Old Covenant context. Under the Old Covenant God demonstrated his love, election, and sovereignty by blessing his people with offspring, land, and wealth. In a similar way, the New Testament witnesses to the reality that in sending Jesus, God has blessed his people with the perfect and promised offspring of Abraham, the King who will rightly rule his land, and the most precious of all possessions. The promise of world-wide blessing bestowed upon Abraham has been fulfilled in that "those who are of faith are blessed along with Abraham, the man of faith" (Gal 3:9 ESV). God's universal plan to bless all the nations that he initiated in Gen 1:28, 9:7, and 12:3 is manifested in the New Testament as the message of the gospel going to the ends of the earth. Those who have Jesus have God's promised blessings.

This is why Paul can say, "He who did not spare his own Son but gave him up for us all, how will he not also with him graciously give us all things?" (Rom 8:32 ESV). In Eph 1:3 (ESV) we read that God "has blessed us in Christ with every spiritual blessing in the heavenly places." If you have placed your faith upon Jesus Christ and united with him in his death and life, there is nothing that is good for you that will be withheld. As members of the New Covenant community, earthly blessings are still very real and we know that "every good gift and every perfect gift is from above" (Jas 1:18 ESV). But on this side of the cross we understand that God's blessing, now manifested in Jesus, is not measured by how many good things we get in this life—whether money, health, houses, or children. Many missionaries throughout the centuries have indeed cut off the blessings of modern healthcare and comfortable living to take the Gospel to remote parts of the world. Some of those missed blessings were no doubt large families with beautiful children. The Apostle Paul writes in Phil 3:8 (ESV): "I count everything as loss because of the surpassing worth of knowing Christ Jesus my Lord. For his sake I have suffered the loss of all things and count them as rubbish, in order that I may gain Christ." Having children is a wonderful joy, privilege, and blessing that God has bestowed upon humanity, but sometimes this good gift may be passed over for the sake of gaining and giving Jesus. This is not birth control for the sake of convenience; it's birth control for the sake of a calling.

Raise Up Spiritual Children

The Apostle Paul expands his view of family with a post-resurrection perspective that sees the family of God as those who have been united with Jesus in faith. As a single missionary, Paul never had physical children. But he repeatedly refers to his disciples and co-workers as his children on behalf of their common faith in the gospel. Therefore, whether married or unmarried, the argument can be made that the Bible does instruct all believers in the gospel to raise up children in the faith. The Apostle Paul addresses three of his spiritual children in his pastoral letters—Timothy, Titus, and Onesimus. He writes:

> To Timothy, my true child in the faith ... (1 Tim 1:2 ESV)
> This charge I entrust to you, Timothy, my child ... (1 Tim 1:18 ESV)
> To Timothy, my beloved child ... (2 Tim 1:2 ESV)
> You then, my child, be strengthened ... (2 Tim 2:1 ESV)
> Titus, my true child in a common faith ... (Titus 1:4 ESV)
> I appeal to you for my child, Onesimus, whose father I became in my imprisonment ... (Phlm 1:10 ESV)

Paul's reference to his spiritual begetting of Onesimus while in prison likely refers to his conversion to Christianity. It follows then that Paul would encourage women and men in the church to do the same work of proclaiming the gospel and training up younger believers in the faith (Titus 2:1–5). The conclusion for the family of God is summed up well by Kathryn Blanchard when she writes: "Christians with children are never free to be isolationist with regard to their families; nor may child-free Christians conclude that the needs of other people's children are not their problem."[8]

When is It Right to Limit Having Children?

If the Bible does allow for Christians to limit the number of children they have, we must ask: How do we determine when the quiver is full? The answer is that the Bible does not give us a set number, and I'm incredibly thankful

8. Blanchard, "The Gift of Contraception," 242.

it doesn't. While it is true that the Bible is undoubtedly pro-children; it is also *pro-wisdom*. The Bible calls us to walk with a spiritually renewed mind, guided by the Holy Spirit and instructed by his Word. Because we live in a fallen world that is itself groaning for restoration, we are forced to wrestle with decisions that cause us to feel as if we are choosing "the lesser of two evils." So, many around the world face the difficult question: Do I have more children because of the joy and value they bring to me and my family, or do I forsake this blessing because I know that I do not have the means to feed them or take care of them? While on the mission field, I witnessed the consequences of ignoring this decision in cultures—very much like ancient Israel—where the father achieves higher social status with every birth. Children starve and become thieves while their fathers strut through the market because they have *sired* (not fathered) ten children—all the while quoting Ps 127 to questioning missionaries. Not as far from home, I recall sitting in a hospital emergency room with my wife in Louisville, Kentucky listening to young pregnant mothers laughing about how much more beer and marijuana they would be able to buy with their increased welfare checks because their new baby will entitle them to more money. In light of such situations, the words of the Apostle Paul to Timothy are highly valuable: "But if anyone does not provide for his relatives, and especially for members of his household, he has denied the faith and is worse than an unbeliever" (1 Tim 5:8 ESV).[9] In many situations where there are no means to take care of children, the most wise decision is not to have children unless or until the circumstances change.

The word "provide" in 1 Tim 5:8 is quite tricky. What does it mean to provide for a child? Should I have only two children because I can only afford to send two children to a private school that costs $5,000 a year? How we understand the word "provide" often reveals assumptions about out standards of living—some of which are biblical and some of which are not. For parents and soon-to-be-parents, the desire to obey Scripture when planning a family begins by seeking to conform holistically to the message of the Bible with regard to marriage, money, and time. For those of us already in the parenting game, the good news is that every day we have a new opportunity to live out what it means to biblically provide for our children—spiritually and physically. It is a work in progress.

9. The specific context of 1 Tim 5:8 is speaking to the issue of younger family members taking care of the aging members of the family. However, I believe this passage affirms a general principle of family care that certainly applies to parents taking care children earlier in the life of the family.

For many, however, the question about having children is not about the ability to provide for them monetarily. It is: Can I make the sacrifice necessary for them? I recall asking my fifty-something year old guitar teacher when I was in high school why he didn't have any children. To my surprise, he gave an uncomfortably honest reply. He said, "I guess I'm just too selfish. I always knew that if I had kids I would have to spend my time and money on them, and I couldn't buy the guitars and trucks and fishing rods I wanted." Selfishness can lead to unwisely having more children than can be provided for, but it can also lead to never having children in the first place in order to avoid sacrifice. The point is that the number of children is not the central issue in these types of scenarios—it is a question of priority. When the Bible says, "in humility count others more significant than yourselves" (Phil 2:2 ESV), we must respond by making difficult decisions—birth control included—by looking with love to the needs of the other people involved in the decision, whether it is other children, stepchildren, a spouse, or a newly conceived little baby.

Birth Control:
How Do We Limit Having Children Ethically?

Provided that the Bible does not forbid a married couple from limiting the number of children they have, the inevitable question becomes: How can Christians limit the number of children they have while upholding the Bible's portrayal of life beginning at conception? In order to truly address this question we must look at the various modern forms of hormonal contraception. "Contraception, in the strict sense, interferes with the sexual act in order to prevent conception,"[10] but whether or not hormonal treatments accomplish true "*contra*-ception" is debatable, as we will see.

Given the fact that there are currently an estimated 10.7 million women using some type of hormonal contraceptive—and many of those are evangelical Christians—this ethical issue could not come any closer to home.[11] There are currently many different forms of contraceptives: an oral pill (Ortho Tri Cyclean®, Plan B® and many others), injection (Depo-Provera®), patch (Orvo Evra®), dermal implant (Implanon®), vaginal ring (NuvaRing®), and interuterine device (Mirena®). Despite all of these different forms of administration, all hormonal contraceptives act in only a few

10. Curran, "Fertility Control: Ethical Issues," 832.

11. Mosher and Jones, "The Use of Contraception," 7.

ways to prevent pregnancy, and understanding these mechanisms of action as they relate to the menstrual cycle is imperative for this discussion. So, bear with the brief science lesson.

How Hormonal Contraceptives Work

First, a woman's menstrual cycle is regulated by two major glands: the pituitary gland and the hypothalamus. The hypothalamus begins the process by sending neurochemical signals to the pituitary gland. These signals then cause the pituitary gland to release FSH (follicle stimulating hormone) and LH (luteinizing hormone).[12] In the first part of the cycle, FSH signals to the ovaries to mature an egg and cause the cells around the ovary to begin producing estrogen. This estrogen thickens the endometrial lining, as well as communicates back to the pituitary gland. The pituitary gland responds to the raised estrogen levels by decreasing the amount of FSH production.

Once FSH has accomplished its task, the pituitary gland releases LH, which signals the ovary to release the matured egg.[13] LH then stimulates the production of progesterone. After the estrogen has worked to thicken the endometrial lining, progesterone works to make the uterus lining a lush landing pad for a potential embryo. It does so by creating small amounts of glycogen on the lining for instant nourishment if implantation occurs.[14] If an embryo does not implant, the progesterone level drops suddenly. Without the needed hormones, the enlarged endometrial lining detaches, thus triggering menstruation.

Hormonal contraceptives introduce synthetic steroids into the body that send signals to the hypothalamus and pituitary gland that there is no need to produce FSH and LH. All contraceptives use the same basic active ingredients: a synthetic progestin (which simulates progesterone) and ethinyl estradiol (which simulates estrogen), or various combinations of the two. The way in which these steroids enter the body depends upon the method of contraception.

The introduction of significant amounts (i.e. 50 mcg and up) of estrogen into the woman's body affects the blood estrogen level and elicits a pituitary response. The pituitary gland senses plenty of estrogen in the system and therefore does not produce FSH. This acts to inhibit maturation

12. Cutrer and Glahn, *The Contraception Guidebook*, 87.

13. Pasquale and Cadoff, *The Birth Control Book*, 33.

14. Cutrer and Glahn, *The Contraception Guidebook*, 88.

of an egg and prevents the endometrial lining from thickening. However, in most pills today the estrogen dose is between 25 to 35 mcg. This is not large enough to prevent ovulation *consistently*, and in newer pills estrogen is included primarily to potentiate the action of the progesterone and stabilize the endometrial lining to prevent breakthrough bleeding.[15]

When progestins enter the blood stream, the pituitary gland does not produce LH because of adequate levels of progesterone in the system. Without the production of FSH and LH, there is hardly any chance of ovulation. Both FSH and LH production can also be inhibited by using high doses of progestins, which prevent the production of gonadotropin-releasing hormone in the hypothalamus to prevent FSH and LH production in the pituitary gland.[16] However, it should be noted that progesterone-only contraceptives have higher levels of escape or breakthrough ovulation.

Progestins also act to thicken the cervical mucus. This makes sperm penetration much more difficult and thus reduces the rate of fertilization. Prevention of ovulation and thickening of the cervical mucus are the "best case scenario" mechanisms of action. This is because both of these mechanisms prevent fertilization. One prevents ovulation while the other prevents sperm penetration. However, there is a third mechanism to be discussed.

When estrogen levels insufficiently thicken the endometrial lining, the addition of progesterone further reduces the thickness of the lining.[17] This can be demonstrated by the observable pattern of lighter menses in women using hormonal contraceptives.[18] However, the lining of the uterus is not always thinned to prevent implantation. It has long been observed that hormonal contraceptives such as intrauterine devices irritate the uterus, resulting in inhibited implantation.[19] Here we find the ethical difficulty with many hormonal birth control measures.

It is widely agreed upon that a very small percentage (3 percent or lower) of women become pregnant while using hormonal methods of contraception. Therefore, to some extent, breakthrough ovulation does occur. The debate then revolves around these post-ovulatory circumstances.

15. Apgar and Greenberg, "Using Progestins in Clinical Practice," 1845.

16. Ibid.

17. Despite some denial of this mechanism, secular science seems to unabashedly report this as one mechanism of contraception. For a well-articulated discussion see Wilks, Colliton, and Goodnough, "Response to Joel Goodnough," 103–15.

18. Schrager, "Abnormal Uterine Bleeding," 2078.

19. Mishell and Davajan, *Reproductive, Endocrinology, Infertility and Contraception*, 538.

Hormonal contraceptives act to thin the endometrial lining of the uterus and prevent implantation in the rare case of fertilization. If fertilization occurs, and the embryo travels down the fallopian tubes only to find a chemically altered, inhospitable environment for implantation, can this be considered an abortifacient mechanism?

The Ethical Issues at Stake

As Christians seeking to uphold what the Bible says, the underlying premise of this discussion is the assumption that individual life begins at conception. Therefore, is it ethical to select a form of birth control (e.g. "the pill") that does not *always* prevent ovulation and consequently fertilization, yet prohibits implantation of the embryo? It should be noted that by the time the embryo has traveled the distance of the fallopian tubes to the uterus it is no longer a simple zygote. By this time it has grown into a 150–200 cell structure called a blastocyst.[20] If any medical intervention prevents this embryonic blastocyst from implanting on the wall of the uterus, we have entered into a morally unacceptable situation. And it should be noted that this is the precise means used by emergency contraceptives such as the "morning after pill" and post-intercourse IUDs in preventing pregnancy.

The Argument Supporting Hormonal Contraception

The argument for the ethical use of hormonal contraception is well articulated by Joel Goodnough in an article he wrote in response to Randy Alcorn's book *Does the Birth Control Pill Cause Abortions?* Goodnough states that the oral contraceptive pill (OCP) should not be called an abortifacient because this is not the intended use of the pill.[21] The intended use is to prevent fertilization. Certainly there is a different intention in using an OCP for contraception and RU 486 (the "morning-after pill") to induce an abortion. However, is the intent in using the OCP prevention of fertilization or prevention of pregnancy? When asked, many drug manufacturers claim that the primary objective of the product is to prevent pregnancy.[22]

20. Cutrer and Glahn, *The Contraception Guidebook*, 102.
21. Goodnough, "Redux," 37–51.
22. Mirkes, "The Oral Contraceptive Pill," 11–22.

Therefore, the design, function, and consequences of the contraceptive may override one's benevolent intent.

Using the same data as his opponent Alcorn, Goodnough argues that there is no reason to assert that the "hostile" environment of the uterus observed by OCP users could reduce the likelihood of implantation. This assertion plainly goes against the practice of modern *in vitro* fertilization treatment, which examines the endometrial lining for the thickest location to greater increase successful implantation.[23] Regarding emergency contraception, which simply uses the same progestins in a larger amount, David Weismiller writes, "Endometrial changes make implantation after fertilization less likely and, depending on when the hormones are taken, may be the more common mechanism."[24] However, William Cutrer speculates that if there is enough hormone present to result in ovulation, the same hormone could then act to thicken and prepare the endometrial lining.[25] This disagreement on the data reveals the true state of this debate. Decisive data is not available to answer the most crucial questions in this debate. Dennis Sullivan summarizes the positions of major research groups:

> [T]he American Association of Pro-Life Obstetricians and Gynecologists has carefully studied this issue, and has reached the conclusion that "our knowledge of the truth is incomplete." The Christian Medical and Dental Association holds a similar view: "This issue cannot be resolved with our current understanding." While not drafting a position statement on the issue, the Center for Bioethics and Human Dignity has presented both sides of the debate. All of these organizations support the right of conscience for health care providers to not prescribe or dispense these drugs, if such professionals are concerned about a possible abortifacient effect.[26]

Unfortunately, the absence of data does not result in the absence of a decision to be made. The general consensus is that OCPs generally prevent ovulation and negatively affect the endometrial lining of the uterus.

23. Ibid.
24. Weismiller, "Emergency Contraception," 709.
25. Cutrer and Glahn, *The Contraception Guidebook*, 103.
26. Sullivan, "The Oral Contraceptive as Abortifacient," 193.

A Decision to be Made

The use of hormonal contraceptive methods raises a significant and documentable threat to the individual lives of unborn fetuses. Can this endangerment be justified by the Double Effect Principle employed by Goodnough in his treatment? He articulates five qualifications that must be met for the principle to apply:

1. The act itself must be morally good or at least neutral.

2. The person performing the act must intend the act to be morally good.

3. The good effect must not follow a bad effect.

4. The good effect that is intended must have sufficient moral value to justify tolerating the bad effect.

5. There must be no other way of producing the good effect.

Regarding the first criterion, examining the use of hormonal contraception as Goodnough does, one would say that preventing fertilization by widespread, easy contraception is morally good. Second, let us assume the person is indeed intending moral goodness. Next, prevention of ovulation would precede inhibited implantation. However, upon examination of the fourth criterion, the argument begins to deteriorate. Is widespread, easy, and largely effective contraception a moral justification for the possibility of killing life? Sure, a few lives may be lost, but no more unwanted pregnancies. This argument finally fails with the fifth criterion. Certainly, hormonal contraception is not the only way to accurately prevent fertilization. Barrier methods as well as more modern techniques of natural family planning offer significant options for those opposed to hormonal contraception.[27]

Is Hormonal Contraception Too Slippery a Slope?

If we truly cannot know the exact details about breakthrough ovulation and failed implantation with the use of hormonal contraceptive methods, how then should we move forward? I believe with great caution. When it comes to a human life, I would rather err on the side of caution—the same position I hope a doctor would take when considering my well-being! J. P. Moreland offers a helpful way to approach a decision when risk and

27. Cutrer and Glahn, *The Contraception Guidebook*, 53–69.

uncertainty collide.[28] Let's suppose there are two actions: action A that is not immoral, yet is controversial and action B that is truly immoral. If the situation exists in which action A cannot be differentiated from action B, and thus doing action A could contribute to causing action B, action A should likewise be avoided. The implications for this discussion are as follows:

1. If preventing fertilization by means of hormonal contraception is morally good (or more accurately morally neutral),

2. but by doing so there is an inseparable risk of killing a living embryo (morally evil),

3. then preventing fertilization by means of hormonal contraception should be avoided.

Another Responsible Option

For those who are using hormonal contraceptives for its high level of effectiveness, but also are concerned about the ethical issue of breakthrough ovulation, Cutrer presents a methodology that might help prevent the possibility of the fertilization of an escaped egg.[29] During the most likely time of ovulation, the woman could employ fertilization awareness methods in order to detect whether or not she is ovulating.[30] If ovulation is detected, an alternate form of contraception could then be used. This is beneficial in two ways. One, it helps to prevent the possibility of conception. Two, it provides a substantial safety net were the individual to make an inaccurate assessment of ovulation.

To date, the most effective way of limiting children available to Christians is sterilization (99 percent effective). In a recent report by the Center for Disease Control, approximately 14 million people are using sterilization methods of birth control in the United States (female = 10.3 million; male = 6.7 million).[31] Female sterilization occurs from a procedure called a tubal ligation ("tubes tied"), which now can be performed with a laproscope as an outpatient procedure. For men, sterilization is accomplished by excising the sperm-carrying duct with a procedure called a vasectomy. Like any

28. This is the "Slippery Slope Argument" as articulated by J.P. Moreland in "James Rachels," 84.

29. Cutrer and Glahn, *The Contraception Guidebook*, 109.

30. See Singer, *Honoring Our Cycles*.

31. Mosher and Jones, "The Use of Contraception," 7.

surgical procedure there are potential medical risks associated with both, but currently the most significant side effects to be considered are emotional. Doctors have noted that patients experiencing emotional problems prior to their sterilization procedure have experienced heightened feelings of remorse or regret due to their elected infertility. So, while for many the procedure is non-invasive and effective, couples need to consider the emotional well-being of the person involved before quickly moving toward this option. This is a sensitive issue that should be discussed graciously. If the marriage covenant is characterized by love and selflessness, as Scripture describes, no spouse should ever feel pressured into having a sterilization procedure.

Other ethical methods of contraception include barrier methods and natural family planning. These methods are not as effective as OCPs or other hormonal treatments (hormonal injections and OCPs—93 percent–97 percent effective; male condoms—83 percent effective; periodic abstinence, i.e. the calendar or "rhythm method"—75 percent effective), but when compared to the ethical concerns at stake, we cannot allow pragmatism to overtake biblical principle. Recent advances in fertility awareness methods has made natural family planning a more effective option, but because a woman's desire for intimacy increases during periods of ovulation, this method can become something of a consternation to the marriage relationship if barrier methods are not also used.

Conclusion

I have argued that while the Bible does not prohibit limiting the size of families, it does require doing so in a way that cares for the unborn. From an evangelical Christian perspective, the risks associated with the use of hormonal contraceptives are too great for me to bear. The only way a couple can be completely sure that they are not intentionally putting a fertilized embryo in a potentially harmful environment is to avoid hormonal contraception. Until research can definitively prove there is no breakthrough ovulation with these contraceptives, Christians should avoid hormonal contraception in favor of other less controversial methods of birth control such as barrier methods, family planning, and ovulation detection.

5

Economic Recession

Where Do We Go From Here?

Walter C. Kaiser Jr.

Introduction

Bestselling author Robert Kiyosali summed up the present state of the financial world in this frightening way: "When people struggle financially, they are more than willing to have the government save them, unwittingly exchanging their financial freedom for financial salvation."[1]

Accordingly, when the value of money steadily declines, panic begins to set in and free people will begin to give up one freedom after another to almost anyone who comes along and will promise stability in their currency and security of those funds. But this scenario also sounds hauntingly similar to the first two predictions of what will ensue in the "last days." In a list of nineteen characteristics of that final stage of the "last days" in 2 Tim 3:1–3 (ESV): "people will be lovers of self, lovers of money."

"Self-love" begins when we place ourselves in the spot that God alone should occupy. This kind of self-love can root itself invisibly in our hearts and yet still dominate our thinking and living. Such self-love can be seen in the financial shenanigans of the Bernie Madoffs, the Kenneth Lays, and the Martha Stewarts of our generation. But it also manifests itself in that

---

1. Kiyosaki, *Rich Dad's Conspiracy*, 39.

second characteristic, which is the "love of money." Of course, the Bible never says that "money was the root of all evil," but that "the love of money is a root of all kinds of evils" (1 Tim 6:10 ESV).

The Love of Money[2]

Money in and of itself is good, since it enables persons to buy goods. If we did not have money, we would be stuck with a bartering system, which is awfully clumsy for making modern transactions of business. Furthermore, since we are not able to produce on our own everything we need for our subsistence, we need the use of money to buy and sell, much less to offer to others the products of our own making. In this way, money is a measure of value and money itself will carry that value until we use it to purchase another thing that is of value to us.

This is where government comes in, for we expect every nation to have a currency that has a known value and that has some stability, be it the British pound, the Mexican peso, or the American dollar. Most importantly, we expect each government to be responsible for maintaining the stability of its currency over a period of time. When inflation hits the currency of a country, the value of that currency changes rapidly and thus it becomes almost impossible to buy, sell, or offer any services, for value changes often while the sale or contract is in progress. Governments must not allow the rules to change in the middle of the game, for when this happens the likelihood is enormous that many are going to be robbed of the values they thought were there.

The Causes of Inflation

Usually inflation happens when a country excessively increases its amount of currency. For this reason, many watch the work of the Federal Reserve Board. The monetary base of the country is falsely expanded and the tendency is for the value of the money to decline while the amount of currency needed for the same products is increased to try to recover the former value of the item that is being bought or sold.

---

2. I am beholden for many of the concepts in this essay to Grudem, *Politics According to the Bible*, 261–319.

In order to prevent an overly heated economy, the Federal Reserve usually begins to tighten things up by raising short-term interest rates and reducing the quantity of outstanding bank reserves. But what happens when government spending hits record-setting levels without income or reserves to back up excessive expenditures? Recently, the path taken by American leaders in government has been the unorthodox method of pumping more and more dollars into the system, which is a stimulus for inflation and a form of governmental stealing, as individuals are robbed of the value of their dollars and the face value of the contracts they had out on agreement stretching over a number of years.

The despairing note of the present crisis in the American economy is that neither the Republicans nor the Democrats are willing to face up to the seriousness of the problem, for neither party has offered a workable plan that will address the current national debt, which is just part of the overall international and global debt crisis. This same problem often exists on a state level as well. When courageous leaders—such as Governor Scott Walker of Wisconsin, who offered a budget to solve a $6.3 million state deficit in two years and to present a balanced budget—have arisen, those who mourned the loss of benefits and powers they once possessed are now calling for his removal from office. Apparently they feel that they can continue to live in debt as a state and retain the value of their hard-earned dollars along with the former benefit package, which now is not backed by any dollars or reserves. Here is where moral concerns enter the picture: a biblical view of government demands that politicians directly and promptly address the problem, despite the fact that they may want to claim that they did not create the problem. If families are expected to live within their means and not spend more than they make (surely the traditional wisdom of a former generation), then voters can expect that states and the federal government would be required to do the same. Psalm 37:21 (ESV) clearly teaches that it is "the wicked [who] borrows but does not pay back."

Should We Take from the Rich and Give to the Poor?

The current assumption is that all rich persons have achieved their wealth in an unjust manner, therefore it is altogether proper for the government to take a portion of that wealth from them for federal expenses in the form of taxes. Thus, according to the current cry of some of the media and the current president of the United States, "It is time for folks who make more than

$250,000 per year to pay their fair share in taxes." However, there usually is a remarkable silence on what is meant by the term "fair share." Neither is there a disclosure of what is already being paid in terms of the total tax burden of country.

Of course, there are some rich persons (as well as those in other tax brackets) who have bent the tax codes to their advantage and have given back to the government, in some instances, almost nothing despite receiving huge incomes. But the Bible is just as insistent that the rich be treated as fairly as the poor by the government. Naturally, where wrong has been done, those law-breakers should be punished. However, Scripture calls for an even administration of justice:

> You shall not fall in with the many to do evil, nor shall you bear witness in a lawsuit, siding with the many, so as to pervert justice, nor shall you be partial to a poor man in his lawsuit. (Exod 23:2–3 ESV)

Moreover, it is not all that uncommon for those who are Christian believers, and who would also be classified as being wealthy, have been most open-handed with their wealth. The same could be said for many, who as wealthy secular persons, have given extreme amounts of their wealth to a number of charities for the good of society.

In 2009 *Forbes* magazine listed almost 800 billionaires in the world. Included in this list were such well-known persons as: Bill Gates (Microsoft Corporation), Warren Buffet (Berkshire Hathaway and GEICO Insurance), Larry Ellison (Oracle Corporation), Karl Albrecht (Germany, Aldi Discount Food Markets), Theo Albrecht (Germany, Trader Joe's Grocery chains), and the four Waltons (Jim, Robson, Alice, and Christy; Walmart Stores). Yes, Gates did make $58 billion in 2008 and the four Waltons together made $70.6 billion, but the idea that we should rob the rich to give to the poor violates the commandment, "You shall not steal" (Exod 20:15 ESV). They themselves must give an account to God in the final day just as all the rest of humanity for all that God has given them and for the way they managed it as a stewardship from the Lord.

The cry of the masses to rob the rich and give to the poor is from the philosophy that thinks government should equalize the amount of income and the possessions every person owns. Yes, government ought to step in and provide help for those who have fallen on desperate times, especially in assisting them in obtaining skills and an education that will eventually help them earn a living. Nothing in Scripture, however, justifies government doing so by stealing from the rich until an equal amount of money is owned by all. Employers are obligated to pay what is fair and just, but nothing demands that all work is to be rewarded with the same amount of money. This view has more in common with Marx's and Engels' view of communism than it has in common with Scripture.

The Benefit of Lower Taxes

Taxes are one of the main sources of a government's source of income. But the amount of these taxes holds the key as to whether an economy will grow or stagnate. Some would like to deny government all income from taxes, but they should also not expect any services from government, which is ridiculous in our society. Others would argue that the majority, if not all, of our income should be handed over to the government and the government should keep us and take care of everything, which is the argument in large part for socialism. But in this second scenario, individuals can do a better job of spending their income, with less being dispersed on management of the funds, than the option of placing it all in the hands of officials who will do the spending for us and who will in turn offer the services we wish to have, but at high administrative costs.

The argument here is that lower tax rates create more economic energy, which in turn produces a greater flow of revenue to the government. This idea has come to be known as the "Laffer Curve," but has usually been greeted by the media and the general public with skepticism. However, it has been shown to have worked, especially during the Reagan years. When it was fully implemented in 1983, the Reagan era ushered in twenty-five economic golden years, with only two minor recessions in those twenty-five years. Contrast these twenty-five years with the twelve years previous to Reagan's administration, in which there were four recessions, two of which were significant.

So what was it that Reagan did to achieve such economic health during that period of twenty-five years? First of all, according to Phil Gramm, Reagan cut the *top* tax rate from 70 percent to 28 percent.[3] Despite these

3. Phil Gramm was a member of the U.S. House of Representatives from Texas's sixth district from 1979–1985 and a U.S. Senator from Texas from 1985–2002. Previously, he taught economics at Texas A & M University from 1967–1978. Currently he is vice-chairmen of the Investment Bank Division of UBS. He has earned his B.A. and doctorate degrees in economics from the University of Georgia. The material here, including the biographical details mentioned above, is gathered from his October 3, 2011 speech

lower rates, the rich still ended up paying a greater share of the total taxes, viz., 18.3 percent of the total income tax collected by the IRS in 1979. By 2006 the rich were paying 39.1 percent of all the income tax revenue. To quote Gramm:

> The top ten percent of earners in 1979 were paying 48.1 percent of all taxes. By 2006, they were paying 72.8 percent. The top 40 percent of all earners in 1979 were paying 85.1 percent of all taxes. By 2006, they were paying 98.7 percent. [Meanwhile] the bottom 40 percent of [all] earners in 1979 paid 4.1 percent of all taxes [and] by 2006 this same group was *receiving* 3.3 percent in direct payments from the U.S. Treasury.[4]

In the twelve years prior to the Reagan program, economic growth in the U.S. averaged 2.5 percent, but in the following twenty-five years it averaged 3.3 percent. During those same twelve years, America created 1.3 million jobs per year, but during the twenty-five years of Reagan, America added two million jobs per year so that by 2007 there were 17.5 million more Americans at work.[5]

Phil Gramm admits some mistakes were made in the Reagan era. For example, good politics dictated that the number and amount of income tax deductions should be raised, but this had the effect of removing 50 percent of the Americans from the tax rolls. Gramm thought everyone should pay some income taxes.[6]

But it is not all about money and GDP (gross domestic product), for *character* counts just as much. In order to validate this assertion, Gramm calls our attention to what has been happening among Greek civil servants recently. Those who were the victimizers were acting like they were the victims in Greece. The result was the near collapse of the Greek monetary system, which needed a lifeline from the other banks in Europe. The Greek crisis thus demonstrates the inherent need for integrity and honesty at the highest levels of government.

---

delivered at Hillsdale College and published as "Reaganomics," 1–3.

4. Gramm, "Reaganomics," 2.

5. Ibid., 3.

6. Ibid.

Should We Tax Corporations at Higher Rates?

The assumption is that corporations make a lot of money, so why don't we ask them to bear a heavier share of the burden? But this again is just a variation on the assumption that we can take money from the rich and that will solve our problems.

This assumption, however, is false, for what the corporations do is simply pass on to the consumer that increase in the form of higher prices for their product. Thus, it becomes only another form of taxation for everyone. Taxes on corporations hurt ordinary people.

The fact is that the Unites States has the highest taxation rates for corporations of any other nation in the world (with the sole exception of Japan, which is slightly higher). Corporate taxes are at the 39.3 percent level (an average that combines federal and state taxes together), with some states claiming even higher taxes (California, Iowa, New Jersey, and Pennsylvania).[7] Yet, running counter to this trend is a serious note in the *Wall Street Journal* in 2008:

> Over the past eighteen months, nine of the thirty most developed nations . . . from Israel to Germany to Turkey—have cut their corporate tax rates. Nations are slashing rates to attract capital and jobs from the United States, and the tragedy is that our politicians keep making it easy for them [to be competitive].[8]

The way to go is not to demonize big corporations or to make incorrect charges, such as those we hear from time to time that x percent of the big corporations paid no income tax at all that year. But when the truth is learned, the failure to pay income tax is because those same corporations usually posted no profit for that year either.

Suggested Solutions

A first principle must be that all who earn an income should pay some tax that year. If no income is earned for the year, then it is understandable that there is no ability or requirement that a tax be paid.

A second principle is this: The tax code has been tinkered with enough; it is time to go to a flat rate rather than try to adjudicate all the deductions.

7. "America the Uncompetitive," 814, as cited by Grudem, *Politics According to the Bible*, 289.

8. Ibid.

Nearly half of all Americans (47 percent) pay no income taxes at all because they worked the system so well that their deductions took care of all that they owed. This ends up being unfair. There ought to be a simple list of deductions that would benefit society at large, such as giving to charities. All other deductions that would not reduce federal involvement for society should be ruthlessly cut from the code and we should move as quickly as possible to a flat rate tax.

A third principle is that a priority ought to be placed on job creation and skills education for those who need to be upgraded. President George Bush's economic policies, by way of contrast, set a record of fifty-two straight months of job creation, in which the DOW went to 13000, the GDP to 3.5, and a 4.6 percent unemployment figure were the numbers set in that period. Compare this to the situation since January 3, 2007, when the Democrats took over the House and the Senate as the 110th congress, gaining a majority for the first time since the end of 103rd congress in 1995. The new administration suddenly dumped five to six trillion dollars of toxic loans from Fannie Mae and Freddie Mac on the economy. President Bush had asked congress seventeen separate times to stop Fannie and Freddie, beginning in 2001, but his requests were blocked by Barney Frank, head of the House Financial Services Committee, who called such requests a "Chicken Little Philosophy." As we now know the sky did fall and it is still falling.

A fourth solution that is often raised these days is to place one half of one's personal savings in gold. Some feel that a final collapse of standard government response of printing more money and expanding credit is doomed to fail. It is just unthinkable that the federal government can be relied on to provide for the continuing needs of all her citizens when so much of the productive economy (almost 30 percent currently) is transferred to non-producing entities (such as government employment). This means that governments world-wide are severely handicapped in being able to respond to the present crisis when the known solutions have been used for almost 100 years, but they have been exposed as false solutions now that things have come to the present impasse.

The issues presented by the economy are most complex and not easily resolved, but to waste time and energy trying to fix blame is certainly not the appropriate action either. The most important actions, however, will be to cut federal spending at key areas, where we can no longer afford them, and to reduce taxes on individuals and corporations, thus increasing the financial returns for the government, and to severely reduce printing money and extending frivolous credit.

6

Blessed Insurance

How Can Health Care be Healed?

Matthew Arbo

Introduction

"And a woman who had a flow of blood for twelve years and had spent all her living upon physicians and could not be healed by anyone, came up behind [Jesus] and touched the hem of his garment; and immediately her flow of blood ceased" (Luke 8:43 RSV). We find conveyed in the verses that conclude this brief story a sense of profound desperation on the part of this unnamed woman. So many years and so many unsuccessful treatments have passed her by, yet she resolved that if she can but touch the edge of Jesus's garment she will be healed. Miraculously her faith is confirmed; she is made well and told to "go in peace" (Luke 8:48 RSV).

Do we not know friends or family who suffer afflictions, often many years at a time, for whom treatment absorbs their resources and yet no definitive cure is found? The hem we reach out for through prayer sometimes heals and sometimes does not. God's reasons for healing are shrouded in mystery. Yet we must nevertheless reach out! The primary insight to be drawn from this narrative in Luke's Gospel, and indeed many of Jesus's healing miracles, is that the Christian moral vision for health care proceeds from a commitment to the basic dignity of every human being. Jesus demonstrates this truth throughout the Gospels, "healing every disease and every infirmity among the people" (Matt 4:23 RSV).

Likewise, as we think more clearly and carefully about both *why* and *how* health care is provided in the United States, we must bear in mind that a properly evangelical commitment to health care will seek always at every juncture to bear faithful witness to the Healer. In what follows, therefore, we will review several contemporary public health issues, especially those concerning delivery methods, and then identify a few key challenges emerging from a uniquely Christian understanding of health. Those challenges will include topics pertaining to who deserves treatment, the methods used to deliver treatment, and where the ambitions of medical science should be cautiously retracted. To retain focus on these particular items we shall want to skirt many of the complex moral problems treated in the academic discipline of bioethics. We are more concerned here with contemporary public policy debates over health care coverage and the moral principals medical practice should observe. The descriptor, "health care," implies that care of patients should be healthy and that health should be cared for; the question for our purposes is then how a *Christian* ethic illumines that truth. Let's begin though with a few of the problems endemic to public discussions over health care, which we'll then later contrast with distinctly Christian understandings of care.

Contrasting Models of Health Care

As of late June 2012 the matter of universal health care has now been settled. The U.S. Supreme Court upheld the constitutionality of the Obama administration's keystone legislative achievement, the Affordable Care Act, on grounds that its individual mandate should be interpreted legally as a tax. Claimed Justice Roberts in his opinion, "if the mandate is in effect just a tax hike on certain taxpayers who do not have health insurance, it may be within Congress's constitutional power to tax."[1] And so the Affordable Care Act was upheld and will take effect gradually over the next five to ten years as intended, minus certain Medicaid expansions struck down by the court in the same decision. Thus the basic moral question of *whether* everyone deserves access to health care has now been answered politically and legally with a resounding "yes!" The church's prolonged failure to voice the same

---

1. Roberts, National Federation of Independent Business v. Sebelius, 32.

full-throated "yes!" well in advance of this legislation is uncomfortably in-
dicting. Consider a case:

Dennis was terminated from his position at the local plant when the
financial crisis unleashed its worst in autumn 2008. A visit to the family
doctor for a routine check-up two weeks after his termination carried the
unexpected prognosis that Dennis had acquired advanced colon cancer. He
could not afford the cost of aggressive radiation regimens and was denied
coverage by all insurance companies on grounds of having a "pre-existing
condition." The Affordable Care Act, among other things, prohibits insurance providers from denying coverage on the basis of pre-existing conditions. This and many other provisions of the bill, like requiring providers
to word policies in "plain-language," are commendable. No self-respecting
person would deprive another person of treatment when such treatment
is readily available. Health is something Christians want others to enjoy to
the fullest. The deliberately deceptive language of insurance policies, too,
warrants correction, even if the trickery is less notorious.

The more vehement debate at present is over appropriate *methods* for
funding and delivering health care to the public. Two views on the method
of health care delivery are apparently without competitors in contemporary
debate: (i) either care is funded and facilitated by the State, or else it (ii)
continues (by and large) to be provided by private entities. A good example
of state-facilitated healthcare is the United Kingdom's National Health
Service (NHS). Under the NHS every UK resident has access to medical
care, prescriptions are heavily subsidized to the point of making the com-
monest ones free of charge to the patient, and for the most part Britons
are quite satisfied with the quality of their system. Nevertheless, like any
other state-operated entity of this scale and importance, inefficiencies and
excesses are readily observable. NHS physicians take consultations in quick
fifteen-minute increments, many departments are frequently understaffed
or under-resourced, and many unnecessary cosmetic surgeries, adult sex
changes being one example, are performed with considerable regularity.
The NHS is of course only one model of state-operated health service, and
the merits mentioned above only offer a glancing image of how this vast
system works. It is worth pointing out as an aside that the Affordable Care
Act is *not* an unparalleled step toward medical nationalization; it simply
asks those who do not carry health insurance to do so or else pay the required tax.

Privatized health care as currently displayed in the U.S. model is multi-faceted and cyclical. Whereas the nationalized system operates under the singular umbrella of a governing bureau, the U.S. private system consists of several entities, each making its appearance on the stage of treatment at a different time. Suppose you strain your knee while exercising one morning. If you have insurance you will likely make an appointment with your family physician for examination. After your visit the physician's office bills your insurance for a considerable sum, even if the doctor visits with you for only a few minutes, and then will likely bill them a great deal more for all the x-rays and scans required to ensure "due diligence." More cynical commentators have claimed that physicians who submit patients routinely to scans do so only for profit. This is a dubious accusation. Physicians recommend scans both because they wish to make a correct diagnosis and because if they fail to do so and something goes badly wrong they can be held legally liable for their misjudgment. A surplus of successful medical malpractice suits in the past few decades has forced increased compliance standards on physicians that have in turn sent health costs soaring. Thankfully, however, in your case the x-rays and scans return negative—it's just a sprain—and you are prescribed some powerful pain relievers. If you have prescription drug coverage, the prescription provider (and by extension the drug manufacturer who supplies the provider) will also bill your insurance a considerable sum. And yet that's still not all, the physician has also recommended several weeks of physical therapy, which your insurance will not cover and as a result you are required to forego. At least, in the end, you were able minimally to get a reasonable diagnosis of your injury and supplied medication to alleviate pain.

The trouble with comparing these two competing models of public health care is that the purported conflict between them is plainly false. The popular idea that America faces an ideological crisis over health care provision is wildly exaggerated and mistakenly imposes an irreconcilable contrast between each model. Genuine either/or choices are few and far between in life, and the same applies here. Weighing the relative merits of each model often proves a fruitless (e.g., consequentialist) endeavor for decision making and is in any case entirely beside the point given that the U.S. government is not presently capable, nor will it become capable anytime soon, of supplying comprehensive health care to the American public. The federal government might buttress or revise how it subsidizes the cost of health care, but the actual delivery of treatment in all its stages will continue to follow private channels for the foreseeable future.

In this way current disagreements over health care *delivery* options distract from the more pressing issue of how *rightly* to reform lingering injustices in health care. Emerging support for a nationalized system is attributable in part to deficiencies of the private system itself. The seemingly inseparable health care trinity—doctors, insurance companies, and other manufacturers (especially pharmaceuticals)—sometimes convey the troubling impression that each industry is out to exploit the other for maximal revenues, which patients are then forced predictably to underwrite. This was illustrated by your visit to the doctor for treatment of your sprained knee: the physician, insurance company, and pharmaceutical manufacturer find ways of exploiting one another for added revenues. Unfortunately, the mere perception of exploitation has in many instances now deepened into outright public suspicion; the system itself is often thought to be intrinsically exploitative. Widespread frustrations over systematic injustices then descend rapidly into all sorts of confused rhetoric, mostly angry and unsubstantiated. None of this is to suggest, of course, that the current system is without serious faults. The distressing cost of health care itself, compounded by the federal government's dedication to subsidize many of these costs, is perhaps reason enough to view the present system as fundamentally compromised. But this cost is merely one problem among many.

Renewal of Institutions

Getting some distance on false debates and on the entrapping frustrations they often produce, we may begin to detect the public's real concern: justice. Replacing one system of care with a newer, favored system does not guarantee greater justice. In fact, as Edmund Burke suggested in the wake of the French Revolution over two hundred years ago, this sentiment often belies unwarranted commitment to revolutionary change for the mere *sake* of revolutionary change.[2] Novelty is an alluring but deceptive object. No, the better, and indeed *Christian*, reappraisal of health care must ignore bickering over delivery systems and attend cautiously to the problems endemic to the motivations, means, and ends of health care and then (if possible) propose judicious remedies to those problems.

2. Burke, *Reflections*.

If we believe Paul's instruction in Rom 13 that civil authorities are appointed by God to restrain evil on earth, then modern Christians may reasonably expect civil authorities to help create conditions for social flourishing, including the punishment of wrongdoing. Every Christian desires freedom to live faithfully before God and generously with others so that when a perpetrator wrongly disrupts that order the state is expected to *right* the violation and restore order. Law exists precisely for this reason; it structures and guides political authorities in the enforcement and application of justice. To that end many have prayed throughout Christian history for the judgment of rulers to be clothed by law.[3]

This understanding of political authority as protector of civil order and corrector of injustice means that Christians may voice prudent concerns over the rightness or wrongness of a specific health care issue and advance rationale for those concerns as needed. This is one of many purposes served by political institutions. Of course, in addition to voicing such concerns we may also *act* to rectify a problem directly ourselves. In doing so we are contributing to the vital renewal of institutions, and in this case to the *healing of health care itself*. Renewal on this scale requires patience and unbending tenacity, but in what follows allow me to offer examples of specific "wounds" afflicting current health care provision and a few "remedies" that might serve to mend them up. For the sake of convenience we'll call these wounds (i) cost and (ii) procedure. It should be added that these examples are by no means comprehensive and will only sketch a partial picture of what institutional renewal might look like; in fact, the urge for comprehensiveness is precisely what I want to resist.

As mentioned above, the exorbitant *cost* of health care is perhaps the system's most glaring wound. Root causes for this inflation are numerous and recounting them would deserve its own essay, but let me nevertheless propose a few potential remedies so as to honor my promise. First, increasing the quantity of physicians nationally would bring greater balance to the supply and demand ratio (more doctors for fewer patients) and offset some significant patient costs. One reason for current imbalance is the fixed number of medical schools authorized by each state and thus the quantity of graduated medical practitioners has remained comparably static with respect to public demand. According to recent estimates from the Association of American Medical Colleges, the U.S. will have 62,900

3. For an excellent sourcebook containing reflections along these lines see O'Donovan and Lockwood O'Donovan, *From Irenaeus to Grotius*.

fewer doctors than needed by 2015 and nearly twice that number by 2025.[4] Adding to the stockpile of physicians without compromising the quality of care would thus do wonders for alleviating costs. Second, state legislatures and judiciaries would do well to gradually introduce precise tort reforms. To oversimplify an inordinately complex concept, the proposal here as regards health care is to narrow both the possible damages a plaintiff might sue for in medical malpractice cases, while also prohibiting insurers from denying claims as a matter of policy. Reform of this kind will be painfully slow and realizing even minor goals will feel impossible, but the most difficult tasks are sometimes the ones most needing done, and this is one of them. Lastly, and finally a simpler remedy: a greater emphasis on personal diet and fitness. Despite their decreased proclivity for substance abuse, particularly alcohol and tobacco, eating habits among many American Christian demographics are generally very poor. To illustrate, a report given at the 2006 Southern Baptist Convention from the denomination's health insurance servicer, GuideStone, indicated that 70 percent of those tested during the annual meeting were at "a medium-to-high risk for cardio-vascular disease."[5] More broadly, according to studies sponsored by the World Health Organization, lifestyle diseases account for the deaths of between thirty-six and fifty-seven million people globally each year.[6] Christians have an opportunity therefore through maintaining healthy diets and routine exercise to demonstrate what a healthy life looks like; an initiative that would honor the temple of God and, by extension, lower health costs for the greater populace.

Another wound afflicting the delivery of health care at present is observable in the culture of medicine itself. We have all become aware of morally questionable procedures like sex change operations, body part cloning, abortion, genetic enhancement, and physician assisted suicide, to name only a few. Without much contrivance we can distill the moral complications embodied in these procedures to the *telos*, or designed aims, of medicine. Consider the following excerpt from the ancient Hippocratic oath:

> I will follow that system of regimen which, according to my ability and judgment, I consider for the benefit of my patients, and abstain from whatever is deleterious and mischievous. I will give no deadly medicine to any one if asked, nor suggest any such counsel;

4. Lowrey and Pear, "Doctor Shortage," para. 2.

5. "Hawkins Reports," para. 9.

6. The study from 2008 has not flagged noticeably. See Boseley, "UN Calls Summit."

and in like manner I will not give to a woman a pessary to produce abortion. With purity and with holiness I will pass my life and practice my Art.[7]

Pagan though they are in origin, these commitments to abstain from what is "mischievious," to "give no deadly medicine" (including abortion!), and to practice the art of medicine with "purity" and "holiness," for example, strike many of us as admirable and worthy of acceptance. Indeed, perhaps many modern physicians would also roundly affirm such an oath, although obviously on the cultural level some of these commitments have been altogether jettisoned. The question, of course, is how the *culture* of modern medicine has over time misconstrued the purposes of treatment. Is there an interesting difference between the ancient and modern physician?

Modern medicine has come to favor what we might call an "escapist" conception of treatment. The widespread assumption is that patients require *delivery from* their affliction, a delivery that if closely followed will distance the patient from their suffering and, as much as possible, seek to relieve them from debilitating human limitations. In other words, modern medicine has in theory and in practice taken aim at overcoming the contingencies of human being itself. As the mid-century Christian ethicist Paul Ramsay has lucidly pointed out, bio-chemists that have come to tyrannize the frontiers of medical exploration seem only to insist upon "man's improving self-modification."[8] The enormous promise of medical science has induced a subtle shift "from doctoring primary patients to doctoring that non-patient, the human race."[9] The contrast between the two aims is stark, for one aspires to embodied treatment of the person and their need where the other is to control human biology. Now, should that claim sound overly bombastic, I should remind the reader that geneticists are now but moments away from providing expecting parents the choice of offspring chromosomes. Designer babies are around the corner. Genetic selection is the medical tomorrow.

Basic human suffering antagonizes the optimism inherent to this kind of medical science because it reminds us of our feebleness and of our failure to "escape." Says Stanley Hauerwas: "the sick constitute a threat to us by making us aware of the frailty of our own connectedness, the thinness of

7. Hippocrates, *The Oath*, para. 1.

8. Ramsay, *Fabricated Man*, 121.

9. Ibid.

our shield of reason, and the limit of our control over the world."[10] Unbearable as it may be, suffering is thus absolutely *vital* to living a richly textured life. The incarnation and crucifixion of Jesus Christ in fact validate the importance of suffering, for by it he familiarized himself with our sufferings. Perhaps in severe anguish a patient may require medical relief of sorts; that much can be conceded without compromising the attending reminder that not *everyone* who suffers pain *always* needs absolute relief from it. Christians would therefore do well to remind the world that medicine is for treating patients, and to the extent that it aspires to controlling life's biological contingencies should resist pandering to idols.

Conclusion: Affirming the Healer

The account of the woman with bleeding that began this inquiry captures marvelously both the promise and limitation inherent to the practice of medicine. Its promise is demonstrated in the treatment of needy patients. Who among us has not benefitted from superior surgical instrumentation or from antibiotics? Likewise, who among us, when gravely ill, has longed for some archaic superstition or bizarre alchemy? The vast majority of medical advances have either saved or improved the quality of public health; it would be senseless to downplay the genius of those achievements. Paradoxically, however, the promise of medicine is also the source of its limitation. As modern medicine gains ever-*greater* public influence it offers ever-*fewer* moral justifications for its ambitious aims or for the methods used to achieve those aims. Genetic manipulation is only one example of this paradox. The claim to have at our disposal the means for eradicating many biological afflictions is acceptable if and only if the means for eradicating those afflictions do not overstep moral boundaries. In other words, if the tests required to perfect the procedures of genetic manipulation (as an example) inflict undue harm on innocent lives, as happens every day with embryonic stem cell research, then the ends (obviously) do not justify the means. Too many of the moral justifications offered by medical scientists in recent decades are issued in precisely these consequentialist terms. Society deserves better, clearer justification for questionable medical costs and procedures than are presently offered. We want to hear how medicine is improving compassionate treatment of patients and in doing so we need also to hear sound moral rationale for those studies and procedures. Admitting

10. Hauerwas, *Suffering Presence*, 49.

that just because something *can* be done medically does not mean it *should* be done would be a great place to start. And this point leads us back again to the case of the woman with bleeding.

Truly evangelical thinking about health care understands treatment as an opportunity to bear witness to the Healer. Spectacular as the "miracles" of modern medicine have been, modern medicine cannot correct the human condition. Human flesh is feeble; from dust we came and to dust shall we all return. Modern medicine will therefore fail each and every one of us in the end, for it cannot save us from our inevitable deaths. That limitation is disclosed implicitly in the narrative of the woman with bleeding. The many physicians she consulted could not cure her ailment and when their competence was expended she reached for her only remaining prospect—the mercies of Jesus. Differences between ancient and modern medical knowledge are irrelevant to the point made here. Health care must be *delivered universally* and *practiced particularly* in a manner that affirms the character of humanity's true Healer. He opened his arms to all the sick and then took that ministry to its ultimate climax by sacrificing himself to heal the sins of the world. His glorious resurrection reveals that real, durable healing comes only by doing what the woman with bleeding did: reaching out in faith to the One who heals every sickness. And praise be to God that is exactly what we are promised in the closing passages of John's Revelation (21:5 RSV), where the Lamb of God declares triumphantly, "Behold, I make all things new!"

7

Right vs. Left

Whose Side is God On?

CORWIN E. SMIDT

Introduction

OVER THE PAST SEVERAL decades, American political life has become far more polarized along ideological lines, with designations of, and differentiations between, political conservatives and political liberals becoming increasingly common within our political discourse. To a certain extent, this growth in ideological polarization is a function of the fact that both of our two major political parties have become more homogeneous over the past several decades, ideologically speaking. As a result, partisan and ideological divisions within American politics reinforce each other today more fully than a half-century ago, with the words "conservative" and "Republican," or conversely the words "liberal" and "Democrat," becoming far more synonymous now than previously.

This chapter seeks to encourage Christians to reflect more deeply about their basic political perspectives and to be more cautious about assuming the correctness of their ideological convictions when making political decisions. Though ideologies help to provide important interpretive frameworks for analysis and assessment, it is important to recognize that ideologies are human creations, seeking to simplify complex social and political phenomena, in order to enable adherents to make "sense of the political world."

It should be noted, however, that the title of the chapter is actually framed improperly for Christians. Rather than beginning with the political divisions within our ranks today and then asking which side God is on politically, we should instead be asking whether we are truly aligned with God's purposes. Unfortunately, all too often, Christians are inclined to make idols out of their ideologies, bowing down to certain perspectives as if they reflected eternal truths and then evaluating one's fellow Christians, not as brothers and sisters in Christ, but by the political positions they adopt.

Certainly when Christians engage in political life, they may do well to employ particular principles, and they may benefit from the use of certain interpretative frameworks of understanding. But, political principles and ideological interpretations are neither religious commandments nor matters of divine revelation. Human thought is always tainted by the adverse effects of the fall and humankind's sinful condition, and, as a result, neither the political left nor the political right can claim the mantel of divine favor. And, if devout Christians seeking to be faithful to their sovereign God "cannot come to an agreement on matters where there appears to be direct biblical teaching (such as the administration of the sacraments or eschatology), it can hardly be expected that they will come to agreement on the matters where biblical teachings are arrived at only indirectly and inductively."[1]

This chapter issues a call to Christians to exhibit greater humility with regard to political life. This call to greater political humility is based on three considerations that will be briefly discussed below. First, given the nature of biblical discussion related to the politics, as well as the need for human interpretation and application of these biblical texts, it is important that Christians adopt a posture of theological humility when engaging in political life. Second, given the complexity of politics, the limited adequacy of information related to political issues under consideration, and the inability to predict with certainty the outcomes of legislative policies, there is a moral ambiguity related to politics that further calls Christians to exhibit political humility when engaging in political discussions and decision-making. Finally, given the biblical command to love one's neighbor as oneself, along with the need to recognize our lack of absolute certainty related to correct theological interpretations and legislative outcomes, it

---

1. Henry, *Politics*, 75.

is imperative that Christians be willing to exercise greater charity to one's political opponents.[2]

The Need for Theological Humility

For evangelical Christians, the Bible serves as the authoritative text and the normative basis for Christian action. Since human understandings and intellectual capacities have been distorted by the effects of sin, evangelicals turn to the Bible as the primary source by which to discern God's will. Indeed, God's revelation to humankind found in Scripture is considered the primary basis by which to measure and test human claims made on behalf of reason and experience—including those related to political life.

However, despite the fact that *sola Scriptura* has long served as the Protestant basis for discerning God's will for humankind, there are a number of complications when applying this principle to political life—resulting in a need for Christians to exhibit a level of theological humility when discussing politics from a perspective that seeks to be faithful to biblical teachings. These three problems relate to (1) the nature of the biblical material related to politics, (2) the need for interpretation of biblical texts, and (3) the effects of sin in interpreting Scripture.

The Nature of Biblical Material Related to Politics

Given the purposes for which it was written, the Bible does not provide some treatise that explicates a particular philosophical perspective related to civic and political matters. Within the Old Testament, the Israelites were first governed by judges and later by kings. Within these institutional arrangements, the opportunities for Israelites to engage in politics were quite limited—if not nonexistent.[3] Nor was political activity an option for the early Christian community. As a result, there was little reason for the biblical authors to discuss the matter in either Old or New Testament writings.

---

2 This argument is similar to one made earlier by Marshall, *Public Square*, xiii. In addition, many of these same contentions may be found in Smidt, "Principled Pluralist."

3. Of course, certain actions while not explicitly political in nature can be deemed as political action implicitly. For example, compliance "with the law" or with the commands of the Old Testament king or the Roman Emperor (or the lack thereof) can be deemed as an inherently political act.

Nevertheless, there are particular biblical passages that do relate to public life, some directly and others more indirectly. But, even those biblical passages that do address civic and political matters must be assessed to determine whether they represent instructions for a particular historical audience (certain statements, for example, may relate specifically to particular kings or kingdoms in the Old Testament) or whether they represent instructions that transcend time and place. Overall, however, it is probably accurate to state that those biblical texts that directly address politics and serve as guides for Christian political action are, in fact, relatively few in number, fairly general in the nature of their discussion, and in need of some level of interpretation with regard to how these particular texts apply to contemporary political life.

The Need for Interpretation of Biblical Texts

The need for interpretation would not necessarily pose a particular problem were Christians in agreement as to how such biblical passages should be interpreted, but these particular Old and New Testament texts have been subject to different theological interpretations. For example, Christians, as a whole, have long held that government is an institution authorized by God. Though governments have been viewed by most Christians as a legitimate institution, the authority that is granted governments is generally viewed as legitimate only insofar as it operates within its "divinely assigned" sphere of authority—as "particular governments or governmental acts may not be [deemed legitimate]."[4] And, generally speaking, Christians view the primary function of governmental institutions to be that of securing justice and pursuing the common good, with the notion of the common good standing at the heart of the social teaching of the Catholic Church.[5]

But, though Christians generally agree that governments are institutions ordained by God that are mandated to pursue justice and seek the common good, Christians are far from united on what the government should be doing in order to fulfill this divine mandate. There are several reasons why this is the case, and the first relates to the fact that biblical texts must be interpreted and inferences made as to what such texts are thought to reveal. For example, one source of divergence in Christian interpretation stems from different theological interpretations related to the broader

4. Chaplin, "Conclusion," 214.
5. Longley, "Government," 160.

93

biblical themes of creation, fall, and redemption—specifically whether or not governments were occasioned solely because of the fall. For those who view government as arising solely on the basis of the fall, the political sphere has largely a negative justification: to restrain sin, preserve order, and engage in corrective justice (the "righting of wrongs"). Though such a perspective does not necessarily imply "minimal government," it does diminish expectations related to what governments are able to achieve.[6]

Other theological interpretations provide for a more positive view of the government. These perspectives generally hold that, even in a sinless world, there "would be a need for some kind of authority that held a legitimate right to have its rules followed."[7] Thus, from this perspective, the function of the state is not simply, following the fall, to hold back sin but to enable "members of society to accomplish more in their life together and fare better than they would simply on their own."[8] Accordingly, this theological interpretation typically leads to "wider conceptions of the scope of common good and justice, thereby potentially legitimizing more government intervention than would the corrective view."[9]

Moreover, other factors also come into play with regard to interpreting biblical texts. In addition to possible theological differences, there are also likely to be differences among Christians in terms of their analytical understandings of such principles as justice, the common good, and equality. Even if all Christians agree that the state should pursue justice, it is far from clear just what that might mean. For example, simply with regard to

6. Chaplin, "Conclusion," 223.

7. Smidt, "Principled Pluralist," 130. For example, even in the absence of a fallen world, different people cannot choose to follow different rules at each intersection where traffic lights are installed; identical rules must prevail across different intersections or chaos would result. Consequently, even in a sinless world, there may well be a need for some kind of state authority that determines for the larger community the particular standards and procedures that are to be followed by those within the community (e.g., where traffic lights should be placed, the rules to be followed related to such lights, and the authority to bind all within the community to obey the rules related to those lights).

8. Ibid., 131.

9. Chaplin, "Conclusion," 224. Christians also disagree as to what extent the church as a body of believers should be engaged in political life. Some Christians contend that the church represents "a resident alien living in the midst of a worldly kingdom," with Christian commitments rendering any substantive engagement in the public sphere between Christians and non-Christians impossible (Ahearn, "Aliens and Citizens," 198, 201). Other Christians, however, contend that "the place of the Christian in liberal democratic society is not that of a resident alien, but that of a responsible, yet critical, citizen" (ibid., 202).

notions of justice, there are different analytical understandings of justice as to whether justice is retributive, distributive, or restorative in nature. Even if one were to restrict one's understanding of justice to simply distributive justice, there are still a variety of understandings as to what distributive justice entails. Thus, even if all Christians believed that governments emerged solely because of the fall and that the primary function of government is to secure justice, Christians can still, given their different understandings of justice, come to different conclusions about the nature of governmental power, how governments are best able to secure justice, and the extent to which justice is likely to be fully realized through state action.

Finally, assessments related to the role of government are also related to other, more empirically related, factors: e.g., one's interpretation of the proscribed powers given by the American constitution to different levels of government; one's assessments of the present cultural, social, and economic realities within American life; one's judgment related to the root causes of problems that are currently confronting American society; and, one's beliefs related to the likely consequences (both intended and unintended) of governmental actions. These various interpretations, assessments, and judgments do not rest on one's theological interpretations or one's analytical perspectives, but they likely shape one's expectations related to the propriety, need, and wisdom of governmental intervention in particular matters of public life.

Given these differences in theological understandings, analytical perspectives, and empirical assessments, it is likely that Christians who seek to be faithful to their Christian calling can easily come to different views related to the role and function of government, the particular political priorities or issues to be addressed, the specific public policies that should be pursued related to such political priorities, and the political party most likely to pursue and implement such politics.

The Effects of Sin in Interpreting Scripture

Historically speaking, evangelicals have generally adhered to an individualistic social philosophy—a perspective that sees structural changes in the institutions of society as not necessarily achieving the greater common good that others may anticipate from such changes.[10] Given the inherent sinful nature of humankind, efforts to transform the social and political

10. Hollinger, *Individualism*.

order are generally seen as being largely futile. Moreover, government and institutional structures themselves are tainted by sin, as they are led and administered by sinful human beings. At best, government may be able to restrain the social manifestations of evil, but it cannot eradicate its root causes, as such causes reside outside its control, within human nature itself. Thus, evangelicals have generally stressed individual transformation as the key to social change, personal morality over social ethics, and a limited state.[11]

However, sin affects all—Christians and non-Christians alike. As a result, sin can affect our interpretation of biblical texts. Thus, throughout church history, it is not surprising to find that sin has distorted even communal understandings of biblical texts (e.g., biblical defense of slavery). As a result, despite what might be longstanding interpretations of biblical texts related to political life, it is prudent that Christians be constantly aware that sin can distort what they believe to be faithful to biblical teachings.

Moreover, it is important to note that this historic evangelical perspective is not directly drawn from biblical passages, but is rather primarily inferred from biblical texts. I don't mean to suggest here that this longstanding evangelical perspective is necessarily faulty or wrong. Rather, my point is that, regardless of even a longstanding tradition of biblical interpretation within one's religious community, there remains a constant need to recognize that the effects of sin may well have influenced these longstanding interpretations of scriptural texts. This human nature of biblical interpretation is further revealed by the fact that Christians living in different places and times have interpreted these texts differently. However, even Christians who live within the same political system at the same point in time have come to read biblical texts differently. Though such differences in understanding may be a function of the fact that sin can shape our biblical interpretations, they may also simply reflect the fact that differences in political judgments can also come into play when seeking to apply these biblical texts to particular political conditions and circumstances. All of this suggests that Christians should always exercise a certain level of theological humility when discussing Christian perspectives related to politics.[12]

11. Ibid., 44.

12. Given this situation, as well as the different historical and environmental contexts within which Christians have found themselves, the political actions of Christians have also been shaped by certain facets of their particular cultural and denominational history.

The Moral Ambiguity of Politics

The need for exhibiting Christian political humility is not solely dependent on our need to recognize the human component of theological interpretation, it is also a function of the moral ambiguity of politics. Though politics is not the only arena of life within which moral ambiguity is present, what distinguishes politics is the *extent* to which moral ambiguity is present.[13]

The Nature of Politics

Conflict stemming from self-interest lies at the heart of politics; this conflict can be seen as a consequence of the fall. But, if conflict is integral to politics, so too is arriving at some consensus (the reaching of some political compromise). Achieving a compromise politically reflects an ability among legislators and citizens to move beyond pure self-interest. Compromise is necessary in politics because the political ambitions of human beings never transcend humankind's selfishness. However, if conflict makes politics necessary; compromise makes politics possible.[14]

This emphasis on compromise as a principal component of politics does not imply that all political values or all political interests are necessarily equally meritorious. In the competition for different political ends, there are inherent ethical assumptions pertaining to the good. Typically, policy differences reflect different assessments related to relative goods or moral ends. In the final analysis, therefore, politics is really a struggle between competing conceptions of the good, hardly ever simply the choosing between good and evil.

Thus, in the political effort to seek public justice, there is a place and need for negotiation and compromise. First, principles must be applied to particular circumstances and changing contexts. Discerning what constitutes justice in these new and different circumstances may well require discussion and negotiation among different parties. Moreover, there may be varying principles that apply to the area of public policy that may well stand in tension with each other. Because, in such cases, emphasizing one principle diminishes another relevant fundamental doctrine (e.g., in terms of American political values, a tension often exists between promoting

13. Henry, *Politics*, 73. This section of the chapter draws heavily from Henry, *Politics*, 59–91.

14. Ibid., 67–72.

freedom and equality simultaneously), negotiation and compromise may be necessary to seek a proper balance between the two principles involved.

Constructing just public policy therefore requires debate and compromise, yet many Christians tend to believe that compromise is an evil thing to be avoided. Christians need to recognize that mutual concessions are a fundamental feature of human life (e.g., within a marriage, spouses frequently have to compromise with each other); it is not peculiar to the political realm.[15] But, even as a political tactic, Christians have frequently been unwilling to engage in the practice of "give and take." Rather than constructing and pursuing a realistic agenda of incremental progress toward the achievement of one's policy goals, many Christians have expected too much too fast. In working to pass public policy that seeks to achieve public justice, the perfect should never become the enemy of the good. One should not view taking incremental steps toward a desired policy goal as constituting unprincipled action.

Nevertheless, there remains a moral ambiguity that surrounds assessments of desirable measures of public policy. Three facets about the nature of politics contribute to its moral ambiguity. First, as noted above, politics frequently relates in part to choosing between relative goods in terms of political ends, and the moral ambiguity of politics relates to the need to decide which of these various relative political goods are more substantial, meritorious, or critical in nature than other such goods. For example, with limited federal revenues, should money be directed to helping the disadvantaged, cure illnesses or address health issues, provide for a common defense, protect the environment, support education? Each of these particular goals has relative merit, but which is more important than the others? There are no clear biblical guidelines in making such assessments.

A second characteristic of politics that contributes to its moral ambiguity relates to the very complicated problems with which politics must deal. Not only are many problems that politics seek to address immensely complex, but the policy decisions on these complex issues must be forged on incomplete, inadequate, and/or ambiguous information. There is always the desire for better data on which to make political decisions, and the data that are available can usually be subject to multiple interpretations. Hence, there is always a cloud of uncertainty surrounding any piece of proposed legislation, with different people being likely to come to different

15. Marshall, *Public Square*, 142.

assessments as to whether any piece of proposed legislation will actually accomplish its intended purposes, rectify the problem, and resolve the issue.

Third, even if there were universal agreement as to which policy area held the greatest priority, what constituted the major problem to be addressed related to this area of public policy, what the data revealed about that problem, and that some proposed piece of legislation would accomplish its intended purposes, there still would likely be differences in assessments related to other, unintended, outcomes associated with such policy proposals. Thus, the moral ambiguity of politics also relates, in part, to the fact that political decisions and particular public policies have both intended and unintended consequences. Neither Christians nor non-Christians can predict with complete accuracy and assurance that the intended outcomes of legislative policies will be achieved nor that certain adverse unintended, or unanticipated, outcomes will not emerge in the wake of such legislation. Even policies proposed and passed with the best intentions and assessments can still foster undesirable unintended outcomes not necessarily anticipated by the passage of such legislation.[16]

The Presence of Common Grace

Likewise, when it comes to political life, it is important to recognize the theological distinction between what might be labeled "particular" grace and "common" grace.[17] While those who are called by God (and who respond to that call) experience a particular kind of grace, common grace

---

16. A good example of an unanticipated consequence of well-intended legislation is that related to restrictions placed on individual and corporate contributions to political campaigns. In an effort to prevent those making large campaign contributions to have undue influence about elected officials, Congress passed the Campaign Finance Reform Act of 1973, which limited the amount of money that individuals could donate to a candidate's political campaign. However, candidates could use as much of their own personal resources as they wished in financing their campaign. The net result has been that those who are less wealthy have had to spend more time raising money for their campaign, as they are forced to raise their money in relatively small amounts across a large number of people, while the wealthy do not have to spend nearly the same amount of time to raise the necessary finances for their campaigns. Thus, as a result, we now have many millionaires serving in the U.S. Senate who had never served in public office prior to their election to the Senate.

17. The discussion in this section of the chapter is drawn in large part from my previous discussion of common grace and its relationship to politics. See Smidt, "Principled Pluralist," 131–2; 145–6.

is that grace afforded to all people regardless of religious belief. As Jesus declares in Matt 5:45 (NRSV): ". . . [God] makes his sun rise on the evil and the good, and sends rain on the righteous and the unrighteous." Thus, there is a "common grace" that all humanity shares which is to be distinguished from God's "special grace" or "particular grace." The common grace of God is experienced in the ordering of nature, the restraint of evil, and the ability of unbelievers to reason and perform acts of civil good. The doctrine of common grace holds that God bestows on humanity a grace that, while not "saving," enables unbelievers to develop many virtues and express many truths.

Therefore, as Christians, we do not believe that all insights and wisdom of, or accomplishments associated with, unbelievers are necessarily bad and are to be rejected as totally corrupt and fallen.[18] Not only can "achievements in politics and scholarship, arts and technology, . . . not motivated by faith . . . still be cherished gifts of God," but cooperation between Christians and unbelievers may be possible and even necessary at times.[19] It is this common grace that provides us with certain shared ground with unbelievers, which gives us a basis for Christian engagement with the larger society.[20]

While God has given the state a separate sphere of authority, its responsibilities do not involve doing the work of the church. In other words, the state is not to be an agent for the propagation of religion or the securing of salvation. Rather, through God's graciousness to all people, he has granted the institution of the state to care for the common interests and general welfare of the people over which it has authority. Here the distinction between particular and common grace sharpens our understanding of the role of the state: it is an agency of common, not particular, grace. Government's role is the mitigation of evil in a fallen world, not the redemption of humanity's sinful nature. Its task is not to redeem its citizens, but to sustain the created order. The role of the state is specific and practical: it must maintain the law and uphold public justice.[21]

This principle is crucial for a Christian comprehension of the state, and several important implications flow from it. First, this understanding precludes any utopian view of politics. The state will not wither away with

18. Meeter, *Calvinism*, 72.

19. Bratt, "Dutch Schools," 146.

20. Muow, *He Shines*.

21. Storkey, *Social Perspective*, 299.

the passage of time nor will governments eradicate all injustices or cure sin. Political activity and state action will never ultimately solve social evils, nor can they provide any hope of salvation. While Christians are called to participate in the task of reconciling, restoring, and redeeming the created order, the kingdom of God will never be fully realized before Christ's return. In the present age, political and state activity may alleviate particular injustices such as slavery and discrimination, and it may even ameliorate some of its root causes (e.g., racism). But political and state activity will never fully eradicate human pride or racism; only when Christ returns to earth will such redemption be fully and completely realized—when there will be a new heaven and a new earth (Rev 21:1).

A second important implication of this view is the need for patience. Our political work as Christians is incremental in nature. As a result, we can support and work to implement laws that more fully, though perhaps not completely, embody Christian values (the "good"), even though there may be other proposed laws that more fully reflect Christian values (the "perfect"), but which have no chance of being enacted and implemented at the time. The need for patience and trust that God holds the future require that the "perfect" should never be the enemy of the "good."

Finally, this distinction also suggests that that the political ideas and policies advanced by non-Christians are certainly worthy of consideration and that they may actually have greater merit than particular policies advanced by Christian politicians. There is no guarantee that the policy proposals of Christian politicians are necessarily more virtuous or efficacious than those proposed by politicians outside the Christian faith.

The Need to Exercise Greater Charity to One's Political Opponents

Given competing values, priorities, and assessments, politics entails the presence of disagreement. And, one of the most important decisions we can make related to politics is the manner by which we choose to treat those with whom we disagree.[22] The American system of government, with its sets of checks and balances, assumes conflicting interests and spirited debate. But, our current state of affairs is such that our political life is undermined by a culture of bitterness and contempt that makes it difficult to achieve any common purpose.

22. Gerson, "Two Reasons."

There is clearly a need for greater civility and charity in contemporary American political life. But why should we exercise such civility toward those with whom we adamantly and fundamentally disagree? On the one hand, there are practical reasons to do so. Public deliberation and persuasion play an important role within democratic political systems, and persuasion is more likely to occur when one's language "is reasonable, judicious and sober rather than aggressive, abrasive, and abusive."[23]

But there are important religious reasons to do so as well. We must treat those with whom we disagree politically with respect because of who they are. Though we may disagree strongly with others, we must never forget they are image-bearers of God and thereby possess inherent dignity and right of conscience. We are to treat others with respect and good manners regardless of their political perspectives. When we treat our political opponents with disdain, we publicly dishonor God.

To treat our political opponents with respect is not always easy. Sometimes the outcomes seem so important, the stakes so high, that we tend to lose sight of the fact that our opponents embody the image of God. As Christians, we need to exhibit a civility that can express strong disagreement as needed without exhibiting personal contempt with one with whom we disagree.

This need to remind ourselves of the humanity and dignity of our political opponents does not preclude rhetorical tough-mindedness. Nevertheless, Christians should be known as much for how they choose to engage in public debate as they do for what they argue. Unfortunately, this is generally not the case today.

The fact that our political opponents are image-bearers of God should be sufficient enough to cause us as Christians to treat them with civility and respect—regardless of who they may be or the particular religion that they exhibit or express. But, we as Christians frequently not only fail to do so, we all too often judge and treat our fellow brothers and sisters in Christ on the basis of the political positions they adopt. Somehow we come to view other Christians who do not hold our political positions as either exhibiting a "less informed" faith or even not a "true" faith in Christ. In other words, we let our political and ideological perspectives make judgments about the nature of someone else's faith in Christ, forgetting that we are not the ones who are to separate the sheep from the goats. Moreover, it is our religious faith that should structure our political perspectives—not the converse. As

23. Ibid.

Paul notes in Gal 3:28, we are all one in Christ; there is no Jew or Greek, no male or female—and, by extension, no Democrat or Republican, no liberal or conservative. God does not judge us according to these distinctions, and neither should we if we seek to be faithful unto him. Rather, as Paul later notes in his letter to the Ephesians: "Put away from you all bitterness and wrath and anger and wrangling and slander, together with all malice, and be kind to one another, tenderhearted, forgiving one another, as God in Christ has forgiven you" (Eph 4:31–32 NRSV).

Conclusion

Christians are called to political engagement; they are not to refrain from politics because it is deemed to be a sphere of activity outside the domain of God's sovereignty. God instituted government for the welfare of humankind. It makes no sense, then, that God would not want his children to be involved in politics. Such an argument would contend that "there is a human institution or structure that God has established and that God intends for human good, but that it is so evil that God does not want his followers to be involved with it."[24]

In terms of the present age, we see through a glass darkly (1 Cor 13:12). Thus, even with the generous tools God has given us in this age to know him and to discern his will (e.g., the Bible and the Holy Spirit), we need to be cautious about claiming to speak for the Lord. As Skillen notes:

> . . . we must constantly act with an attitude of true humility. We should undertake every civic duty, every political action. . .with the avowed understanding that they are not God's will but only our response to God's will. . . .This attitude of humility will lead us to be modest and self-critical in our claims and stated intentions.[25]

Accordingly, one can rightfully state that "modesty and provisionalism" in politics are not reflective of "weak-kneed accommodationism but are required by fidelity to the gospel."[26]

Thus, in the end, ideological perspectives can be useful for thinking about public policy. They can help simplify complex phenomena, organize our political thinking, and provide a starting point when addressing new

---

24. Monsma, "Christian Commitment," 257.

25. Skillen, *Christians Organizing*, 23.

26. Neuhaus, *Public Square*, 123.

political issues. Nevertheless, ideological labels are often the means of reducing real differences to oversimplifications and viewing those who are labeled in a certain way as being all the same. The use of such labels is enticing because it enables one to easily make judgments without the need to engage in the hard work of acquiring knowledge, checking facts, and persuading on the merits of an argument. Moreover, all too often these ideological labels and viewpoints can quickly become impediments to loving God and our neighbors. Thus, we as Christians should be careful about how we use political labels in our thinking and evaluations of others, for:

> Such frameworks offer quick shortcuts for choosing sides on political issues and for selecting candidates. But the quest for ideological purity can supplant the desire to serve God first in our political discussions. Thus, engaging in an ongoing process of self-reflection will help us to determine which is coming first: our Christian commitments or our ideological commitments.[27]

---

27. Black, *Beyond Left and Right*, 50–1.

8

Warfare and Christian Discipleship

Can Citizens of Heaven Fight Wars on Earth?

Thor Madsen

Introduction

THE AMERICAN PEOPLE BELIEVE in religious liberty—or they have so far. They assume that each person has the right to choose his own religion and practice it without fear of government interference. No law may force Muslims to act like Christians, or Hindus to act like Buddhists. We do not use our laws, even in subtle ways, to handicap one religious perspective to the advantage of the others. Trying to do so would cause massive social unrest, and that is one reason why we acknowledge everyone's religious liberty. But there is also a second reason. Christianity influenced our nation's founding more than any other worldview, and Christianity demands religious liberty; so now we have it. Indeed, this liberty of conscience derives from evangelical Christianity's high soteriology, according to which God saves people. We preach, pray, and serve; but he saves them. Therefore, it would be ridiculous to do evangelism with guns or swords. A forced convert is no convert at all. Likewise, we do not compel anyone to bear the fruit of repentance and Christian faith. Those changes must come from regeneration, not regulations emanating from Washington, and thus we come to the matter of just warfare.

If the United States of America were the visible church, so to speak, we would know what to say about bombs and bullets: we may never use them. Our nation represents the Lord before a lost world; and in that case, all 300 million of us should brace ourselves for sacrifice. If the enemy sues for our corn, we would give him our coal as well. If he sinks the aircraft carrier *Ronald Reagan*, we offer him the *Nimitz*. If he makes us pay the *jizya*, we pay him twice as much.[1] Those conclusions might follow, if we were a "Christian nation." But we are not, after all—not in that way, at least—and thus our theory of just war must change accordingly. Three adjustments seem necessary. First, since we live in a pluralistic society and would, in any case, reject compulsory discipleship, no theory of warfare may be accepted which compels all of us to turn the other cheek to foreign aggression. Second, no theory of warfare may be accepted which always keeps Christians at home, secure in their pews, while lost people go off to fight and die. There is something transparently upside down about that arrangement. Third, a theory of just warfare—which might inform national policy—must define our enemies as the whole nation sees them, not as we Christians know them to be soteriologically. In evangelism, the enemy is a person who might become a brother in Christ; but in just war, he is a threat to everyone's life, liberty, and property. We shall adopt the latter description here.

With these caveats in place, we may outline the present argument as follows. There are six claims to be defended. (1) We must decide whether or not warfare is morally acceptable, because we are indirectly responsible for it as voters. (2) Our decision regarding the moral status of warfare must be based on Scripture. We may use secular arguments in support of our theory, but they are logically dependent on Christian premises. (3) No passage of Scripture forbids warfare. While a few of them forbid resistance to evil, this kind of evil is privately suffered and does not constitute a *prima facie* cause of war. (4) Some passages of Scripture condone lethal force when exercised by the state. (5) Pre-emptive and punitive strikes are consistent with biblical principles. They are not forbidden categorically. (6) The dangers faced by our country are real. They are not fabricated or exaggerated merely to serve special interests.

---

1. The *jizya* is a tax imposed by Muslims on non-Muslims.

We Must Decide if Warfare is Morally Acceptable

Our nation will always be at war. As long as this fallen world continues, someone out there will threaten our interests, even our lives. Worse yet, these enemies will hate America with special intensity, as they do now, and we know why. Some of them blame us for their cultural ineptitude. They cannot feed themselves or secure indoor plumbing, and we can. So they envy us for our expertise and prosperity. Others want our wealth and resources; and if they cannot take them by one means, they will do so by another. A third group resents our international reach, wishing that it could duplicate the American influence in science, technology, and entertainment. Finally, we have the Islamists, who claim divine authority to break us under *sharia* law.[2] Or kill us. It makes no difference to them. So we have this choice: surrender or lose our way of life. If we give in, we get peace for a time. Then comes the damage that would look like Sarajevo, circa 1995, if it accumulated fast enough to catch our eye. Or we fight. Either way, we need to know what our options are, and not just tactically. The larger question is moral—whether it is permissible to kill human beings in warfare or, in general, to use lethal force against them—and this one will not go away. As voters, we decide indirectly who dies in warfare and why; therefore, we are responsible.

Just War Theory Must Be Based on Scripture

The analysis offered here will depend entirely on Scripture for its ethical first-principles. We want to know what the Bible says about just war and to shape our policies by it. Of course, this procedure will disappoint some readers who were expecting an argument that even lost people could accept, so that it plays well in the public square, as our nod to pluralism (above) may seem to require. But we have put this latter ambition aside for two reasons. First, it is impractical. We have no space available here to keep the secularist happy along with the Christian. More importantly, the result would be artificial in any case. After all, if there is no God, there are no unjust wars. Indeed, there would be no *just* wars. It makes no final difference what any of us does, in battle or any other setting. Human rights no longer exist, and

---

2. We define "Islamist" as a Muslim who rejects freedom of speech, freedom of religion, and freedom of assembly, affirming only the legitimacy of Islam.

nothing is sacred.[3] Therefore, while our analysis concerns a matter of public policy—and while it respects everyone's liberty of conscience—it will appeal to Scripture as the standard of right and wrong. We have no options, deep down, not if justice concerns human life and suffering.

No Passage of Scripture Forbids Warfare

The Bible contains several passages that could support arguments against warfare because they frown on anger, violence, and the typical causes of human conflict. We gather from these texts that war is an evil business, the sort of thing for which fallen humanity ought to feel collective shame. However, none of them forbids warfare as such or the use of lethal force, whether by Christians or anyone else. On the contrary, the biblical writers balance the two perspectives: we should not live with it, but we cannot live without it. We walk on fallen ground, where the bad and strong hurt the good and weak, if we let them. Therefore, we have soldiers, police, guns, locks, and prisons. Consider, then, the following series of texts which surface in the just war debate. They come from Matthew's gospel, in the main, but our analysis would apply to their parallels in Mark and Luke.

Matthew 5:21–22 (NASB)

> "You have heard that the ancients were told, 'You shall not commit murder' and 'Whoever commits murder shall be liable to the court.' But I say to you that everyone who is angry with his brother shall be guilty before the court; and whoever says to his brother, 'You good-for-nothing,' shall be guilty before the supreme course; and whoever says 'You fool,' shall be guilty enough to go into the fiery hell."

This passage appears to support a pacifist position because it forbids anger, and anger leads to war. If I get angry enough with my enemy, I might just kill him. Warfare also provokes anger, leading to severe acts of retaliation. Therefore, the pacifist could argue that since Jesus forbids anger, he implicitly forbids war. However, the wider context of Scripture prevents us from

3. In fact, reason itself would disappear, if God does; for if a Creator has not designed us to reason competently, we have no warrant for believing that we can apply reason to this question or any other one. Every thought has become a side effect of blind chemistry, as far as any of us would know.

applying vv. 21–22 in this way. One needs only to observe who gets angry in the Bible and why. In the Old Testament, Yahweh fulminates against sinners and sometimes kills them, even on a massive scale (e.g. Gen 6–8; 19; Exod 11, etc.). Jesus drives out the money-changers with an improvised whip (Matt 21:12–13). Then comes the Revelation, where demonic plagues, splitting skies, and lakes of fire terrify the unrepentant (Rev 6–9; 20). From the mouth of Jesus comes a two-edged sword (Rev 1:16), which he uses to "make war" against his enemies (Rev 2:16; 19:21). So Jesus would not forbid unqualified anger, but anger expressed immorally; and in that case, the pacifist reading of Matt 5:21–22 collides with itself. Anger that provokes war is wrong only if war is wrong—which is precisely the question before us.

Notice, then, how Jesus corrects the scribes and Pharisees. They understood the sixth commandment narrowly. It forbids actual murder, they concede, but not the trading of insults and acts of petty revenge. Two men could fight like divas and still qualify as righteous. But Jesus applies the law based on a common sense principle. If God says, "You shall not do x," he also means, "Do the opposite of x." In this case, he means that we should stay on friendly terms with our neighbors, to the extent that we can. So Matt 5:21–22 would forbid warfare only if every case of warfare must, by definition, involve *both* sides in a stubborn refusal to be reconciled to one another; and that is not obvious. In fact, it suggests a moral equivalence behind all cases of warfare, according to which everyone shares the blame. No one is right; everyone is wrong. But this charge dismisses the evidence without addressing it.

Matthew 5:38–42 (NASB)

> "You have heard that it was said, 'An eye for an eye and a tooth for a tooth.' But I say to you, do not resist an evil person; but whoever slaps you on your right cheek, turn the other to him also. If anyone wants to sue you and take your shirt, let him have your coat also. Whoever forces you to go one mile, go with him two. Give to him who asks of you and do not turn away from him who wants to borrow from you."

Pacifists could appeal to Matt 5:38–42 because these verses feature the command, "Do not resist the one who is evil." Thus, if our enemies qualify as evil, we cannot resist them. Instead, we would let them rape and pillage freely, between cups of tea. But this application of vv. 38–42 will not work, given how Jesus illustrates his teaching. The first case involves being slapped, rather than shot, stabbed, or clubbed. In other words, the victim suffers a minor wound. He gets humiliated, of course, as when soldiers press him into service or when someone sues for his tunic. But the aggressor does not hospitalize his victim, nor does he intend to do so. How, then, might the victim respond?

In such cases, the Pharisees would follow the "law of the tooth" (Exod 21:24), understood permissively. If my enemy inflicts a personal, humiliating wound, then by all means, says God: strike back. If he slaps me, I slap him. If he takes my tunic, I will steal his shoes. But Jesus overturns this absurd ruling based on the law's original purpose. The law of the tooth does not permit evil: it *restrains* would-be Hatfields and McCoys. So Jesus disappoints the Pharisees, who expected loopholes; but he goes further still with his disciples. If someone persecutes them, they should accept the abuse: it happens to salt and light. Therefore, if we have interpreted these verses correctly, they would not apply to warfare. The latter involves massive violence, not slaps and insults. It also exposes the Pharisees as hypocrites who lash out when they could stand down. So we move on to further examples.

Matthew 5:43–48 (NASB)

> "You have heard that it was said, 'You shall love your neighbor and hate your enemy.' But I say to you, love your enemies and pray for those who persecute you, so that you may be sons of your Father who is in heaven; for He causes His sun to rise on the evil and the good, and sends rain on the righteous and the unrighteous. For if you love those who love you, what reward do you have? Do not even the tax collectors do the same? If you greet only your brothers, what more are you doing than others? Do not even the Gentiles do the same? Therefore you are to be perfect, as your heavenly Father is perfect."

Matthew 5:43–48 works better for the pacifist, because Jesus actually says, "Love your enemies." Thus we cannot kill them. But the context of vv. 43–48 hinders this application. Verse 47 tells the real story: these enemies have not invaded with siege towers and catapults. We know them personally. We used to greet them in the marketplace, before they offended us. Therefore, we cannot use the mandate, "Love your enemies," against national self-defense, unless we stretch it implausibly.

Indeed, the entire Sermon on the Mount disarms the pacifist because Matthew includes it for apologetic and Christological reasons, rather than as an ethical manifesto (though it certainly teaches ethics). Here we see Jesus issuing decrees with regal authority and confronting hypocrites—just like the real Messiah would, after all.[4] He attacks the pseudo-righteousness of the Pharisees and their self-serving applications of Torah. He also reinforces what the Torah has always required. But if the whole Sermon does that, each part would probably do that; and none would address public policy. These chapters focus on private conduct and rebuke the Pharisees for their exegetical fiddlesticks. They want permission to hate their enemies because they have lots of them and they live next door. Therefore, as a polemic against Pharisaic righteousness, Matt 5:43–48 would not apply to enemies faced on battlefields—not in a straightforward way.

Matthew 26:52 (NASB)

> Then Jesus said to him, "Put your sword back into its place; for all those who take up the sword shall perish by the sword."

During the arrest of Jesus in Gethsemane, Peter draws his sword and cuts off the ear of Malchus, a servant of the high priest (Matt 26:52; John 18:10). We can assume, moreover, that he intended to kill the servant rather than injure him. Therefore, we ask, "What would Jesus do?" Would he accept this defense or reject it; and why, either way? The text answers, in part: Jesus forbids his disciples to fight off the temple guard, giving two reasons for non-resistance. First, he does not need this kind of help. He can call down legions of angels, if he so desires. Second, he intends to fulfill his mission, according to Scripture; and so we get to the point of Matt 26:52: Jesus stops Peter for soteriological reasons, rather than ethical ones. He is not trying to explain what usually happens to violent men—not here. Rather, the Son has a cup of wrath to drink, poured by the Father. He must die on the cross, not by the sword or of old age (John 18:11). Therefore, he forbids violence to defend him—right there in Gethsemane—not as a rule between nations; and thus we cannot use v. 52 to forbid warfare.

---

4. I am grateful to my colleague, Alan Tomlinson, for this insight.

Some Passages of Scripture Condone Lethal Force Exercised by the State

Strict pacifism cannot admit exceptions, because its claims are categorical. No wars are just wars. All warfare is forbidden. No Christian may, at any time, and for any reason, fight in a war. If one backs down from these statements, he becomes a just war theorist of some kind, not a pacifist. Thus we can refute pacifism by catching God either (a) telling someone to fight or (b) condoning the use of lethal force by the state; and he does both. Here are three familiar examples.

Joshua 6:1–27 (NASB)

Now Jericho was tightly shut because of the sons of Israel; no one went out and no one came in. The Lord said to Joshua, "See, I have given Jericho into your hand, with its king and the valiant warriors. You shall march around the city, all the men of war circling the city once. You shall do so for six days. Also seven priests shall carry seven trumpets of rams' horns before the ark; then on the seventh day you shall march around the city seven times, and the priests shall blow the trumpets. It shall be that when they make a long blast with the ram's horn, and when you hear the sound of the trumpet, all the people shall shout with a great shout; and the wall of the city will fall down flat, and the people will go up every man straight ahead." So Joshua the son of Nun called the priests and said to them, "Take up the ark of the covenant, and let seven priests carry seven trumpets of rams' horns before the ark of the Lord." Then he said to the people, "Go forward, and march around the city, and let the armed men go on before the ark of the Lord." And it was so, that when Joshua had spoken to the people, the seven priests carrying the seven trumpets of rams' horns before the Lord went forward and blew the trumpets; and the ark of the covenant of the Lord followed them. The armed men went before the priests who blew the trumpets, and the rear guard came after the ark, while they continued to blow the trumpets. But Joshua commanded the people, saying, "You shall not shout nor let your voice be heard nor let a word proceed out of your mouth, until the day I tell you, 'Shout!' Then you shall shout!" So he had the ark of the Lord taken around the city, circling it once; then they came into the camp and spent the night in the camp. Now Joshua rose early in the morning, and the priests took up the ark of the Lord. The seven priests carrying the seven trumpets of rams' horns before the ark of the Lord went on continually, and blew the trumpets; and the armed men went before them and the rear guard came after the ark of the Lord, while they continued to blow the trumpets. Thus the second day they marched around the city once and returned to the camp; they did so for six days. Then on the seventh day they rose early at the dawning of the day and marched around the city in the same manner seven times; only on that day they marched around the city seven times. At the seventh time, when the priests blew the trumpets, Joshua said to the people, "Shout! For the Lord has given you the city. The city shall be under the ban, it and all that is in it belongs to the Lord; only Rahab the harlot and all who are with her in the house shall live, because she hid the messengers whom we sent. But as for you, only keep yourselves from the things under the ban, so that you do not covet them and take some of the things under the ban, and make the camp of Israel accursed and bring trouble on it. But all the silver and gold and articles of bronze and iron are holy to the Lord; they shall go into the treasury of the Lord." So the people shouted, and priests blew the trumpets; and when the people heard the sound of the trumpet, the people shouted with a great shout and the wall fell down flat, so that the people went up into the city, every man straight ahead, and they took the city. They utterly destroyed everything in the city, both man and woman, young and old, and ox and sheep and donkey, with the edge of the sword. Joshua said to the two men who had spied out the land, "Go into the harlot's house and bring the woman and all she has out of there, as you have sworn to her." So the young men who were spies went in and brought out Rahab and her father and her mother and her brothers and all she had; they also brought out all her relatives and placed them outside the camp of Israel. They burned the city with fire, and all that was in it. Only the silver and gold, and articles of bronze and iron, they put into the treasury of the house of the Lord. However, Rahab the harlot and her father's household and all she had, Joshua spared; and she has lived in the midst of Israel to this day, for she hid the messengers whom Joshua sent to spy out Jericho. Then Joshua made them take an oath at that time, saying, "Cursed before the Lord is the man who rises up and builds this city Jericho; with the loss of his firstborn he shall lay its foundation, and with the loss of his youngest son he shall set up its gates." So the Lord was with Joshua, and his fame was in all the land.

Consider Jericho, which Joshua's armies were to destroy utterly, given the inhabitants' decision to stay and fight, rather than leave and live. For their idolatry, they will now die—the men and women, boys and girls, sheep and oxen—upon Yahweh's orders. The concept of collateral damage does not apply. Not here. Only Rahab and her family survive. Thus we have a *prima facie* case against pacifism: if God requires even *one* war, strict pacifism is in ruins; and he does. Indeed, God sometimes promises to fight right alongside his chosen people, visiting wrath on pagan idolaters; and the entire conquest serves a punitive function.

In response, the pacifist could argue that we have ignored the purpose of these battle narratives. They do not record history, telling us what Israel actually did. They only express God's anger by imagining what might have happened, rather than telling us what did happen. After all, God is supposedly too kind for war. But this strategy falters on two counts. First, the historical narratives of the Old Testament read like history, not fantasy; and thus the pacifist would carry an enormous burden of proof, should he try to deflect the account of Jericho's destruction thusly. Second, the biblical writers assume that their holy God might punish evildoers with violent deaths, either by his own hand or by human weapons. In fact, he does so more often than we think, as noted above. Millions died in Noah's flood. Thousands died in the Egyptian plagues. Sodom and Gomorrah perished in a day. But if this story about Jericho is authentic, strict pacifism is indefensible.

Luke 3:10–14 (NASB)

> And the crowds were questioning him, saying, "Then what shall we do?" And he would answer and say to them, "The man who has two tunics is to share with him who has none; and he who has food is to do likewise." And some tax collectors also came to be baptized, and they said to him, "Teacher, what shall we do?" And he said to them, "Collect no more than what you have been ordered to." Some soldiers were questioning him, saying, "And what about us, what shall we do?" And he said to them, "Do not take money from anyone by force, or accuse anyone falsely, and be content with your wages."

Now consider what John the Baptist says on this topic, or rather what he does not say. In Luke 3:10–17, John describes what repentance would look like, as people anticipate the judgment of God. Verse 11 addresses everyone together, urging them to share with one another. Then he turns to specific groups of people having controversial occupations. Tax collectors ask, "Teacher, what shall we do?" and jaws drop with the Baptist's answer: "Collect no more than what you have been ordered to" (Luke 3:12–13 NASB). Then come the soldiers, who might also have expected rough treatment from this Jewish prophet. "What shall we do?" they ask; and John replies: "Do not take money from anyone by force, or accuse anyone falsely; and be content with your wages" (Luke 3:14 NASB). In both cases, John surprises us, given popular sentiment regarding tax collectors and soldiers. He does not tell either of them to do something else. Rather, they must do their jobs well and justly. In this sense, John's silence is deafening for the pacifist: if war is forbidden, then military service is evil; and John would have said so. He could hardly have done otherwise, given their question. They are asking what repentance looks like for them *as soldiers*. Similarly, as an aside, the exchange between Jesus and the centurion undermines the pacifist's case, given what Jesus does not say (Matt 8:5–13). If all wars are evil, then he would have confronted this soldier, dressed to kill. But Jesus praises the man and nothing else. Again, while this argument draws conclusions from Jesus's silence, it rests on solid ground, given the example that Jesus makes of this soldier (Matt 8:10).

Romans 13:1–6 (NASB)

Every person is to be in subjection to the governing authorities. For there is no authority except from God, and those which exist are established by God. Therefore whoever resists authority has opposed the ordinance of God; and they who have opposed will receive condemnation upon themselves. For rulers are not a cause of fear for good behavior, but for evil. Do you want to have no fear of authority? Do what is good and you will have praise from the same; for it is a minister of God to you for good. But if you do what is evil, be afraid; for it does not bear the sword for nothing; for it is a minister of God, an avenger who brings wrath on the one who practices evil. Therefore it is necessary to be in subjection, not only because of wrath, but also for conscience's sake. For because of this you also pay taxes, for rulers are servants of God, devoting themselves to this very thing.

Finally, we examine the case of Rom 13:1–6, which deals with Christian submission to government, and we may begin by stating the obvious: in the time of Jesus, soldiers carried swords to threaten people with death or to kill them. Swords also projected authority, of course, but only as deadly weapons. Consequently, if Paul describes the secular state as bearing "the sword" (v. 4), it may sometimes kill, in his view, visiting "wrath on the one who practices evil" (v. 4). Perhaps we do not expect Paul to concede as much, given his acquaintance with the vagaries of government action. But he does so on theological grounds. Roman officials did remarkably evil things; yet Paul assumes that God ordains all events, even the rising and falling of emperors and kings. So Paul is not a pacifist, though he would have condemned the wanton brutality of Roman siege warfare, as one example.

Pre-emptive and Punitive Strikes May Be Consistent with Biblical Principles

Many Christian scholars would argue that wars can be just, if at all, only on defense. In fact, a just war theorist could frown on warfare while approving too, by a turn of logic: if every nation confined itself to just wars, we would have no wars at all. No one could fire the first shot. But we reject this boundary for two reasons, one practical, one moral. First, in the modern age, traditional just war theory is unworkable: our enemies would be shelling Topeka long before we had exhausted ourselves at the United Nations; and a WMD-strike would leave us guarding ashes, not loved ones. Thus a defensive requirement constitutes *de facto* pacifism: the "peace" comes when we surrender. If we desire to live, we may have to kill our enemies before they even try to kill us—a hard truth, but a truth nonetheless.

Then the moral question arises, which we can address analogically. Suppose that we have a criminal offender before us, and we wonder how the state should treat him. One group says, "We must do all, and only all, that is necessary to restore him to the family of decent people." The other says, "We must punish him for what he did; and if he also improves by suffering, so much the better." Group A justifies its interference based on the fact that the offender could do better. Group B finds its rationale for handcuffs and prison bars in the concept of deserved harm. He has offended; now let him suffer offense. But notice which goal takes precedence and must do so. The concept of deserved harm leads the way, for without it, we could not justify the remedial steps. Indeed, measures taken to fix the convict might exceed those taken merely to repay what is owed, given the nature of his crimes.

Now consider how deserved harm, as a concept, would apply to whole nations at war. If a nation has given no cause for war—if it deserves no harm—actions taken against it by its enemy would be unjust. Remedial ambitions have no currency in this case. As independent factors, they do not justify warfare. But if our analogy succeeds, then we know what a just war must do first of all. One nation may attack another to inflict deserved harm, not to restore peace or the *status quo ante*. Wars cause suffering required by justice; or they do evil, even on defense. After all, a convict might defend himself against the needle, but he does so unjustly; and when the poisons flow, society is not protecting itself—not before all else. It is doing what justice requires. Thus we fought back after September 11th, but not for prospective gains. Our sorties fixed the Islamists and their repressive governments, but they did something else first: they secured justice for 3,000 non-combatants. In the end, good things also happened to the people of Afghanistan and Iraq; but those side effects only manifest the benevolence of our nation and also our restraint. We also attacked these nations rapidly, as we should. As in criminal law, so also on the world stage: justice delayed is justice denied; and when retribution comes far too late—breaking the link between action and reaction—it becomes an injustice suffered by the enemy himself.[5]

Finally, a word about collateral damage, in light of our previous claims; and we start with a good report. Because of our nation's technological superiority, we can do the impossible much of the time—i.e., inflict crippling damage on a nation's military forces while sparing its civilians. It is well-known, for example, that during the "Shock and Awe" campaign of 2003, life in Baghdad went on, more or less. As a rule, the Iraqi civilians did not fear that our pilots would target them directly or hit them by accident. Nor should they have done so, since our forces behave like men, not savages: they do not kill civilians, once the enemy returns fire. But we face a new adversary nowadays, an enemy which hides in schools and uses children as shields. Therefore, this doctrine of civilian immunity needs a rider that it has always presupposed: justice does not require our forces to spare women, children, the infirm, and elderly, whatever the circumstance. It requires them to spare such people if the enemy removes them from harm's

---

5. This argument is indebted to the analysis of criminal justice given by Lewis, "Humanitarian Theory," 287–94.

way. But if they carry rifles, live near bases, or work in bomb factories, we cannot guarantee their safety.

The Dangers Faced by our Nation Are Real

I have met several people who hate guns and despise the Second Amendment. They regard concealed weapons as amulets for the NASCAR set. But what these critics have in common—to the Jack and Jill of them thus far—is that they live in safe neighborhoods. They do not feel threatened, ever. Not at work, not at home, not when going from the one to the other; and thus it is easy for them to pretend that no one else needs a gun, that defenseless people face no dangers. Likewise, we have among us pacifists of convenience, not principle. They strike fashionable poses, knowing that men with guns will protect them; and we do not engage them here. We write for people who can face the evidence squarely. Yes, some anti-warriors believe that our nation builds weapons only to gratify Dick Cheney and enrich manicured investors. Others believe that we kill our enemies only to take their last ewe lamb. Perhaps we kill for target practice and pride. We hear these theories from the grandly disengaged. But the facts before us tell a different and sadder story. Our nation has enemies who would kill us all, if they could. So do the others, especially Israel. Therefore, we have guns, first to intimidate aggressors, then to kill them should they attack.

Warfare always involves a conflict between sinful nations and sinful people. There are no exceptions. We fight our wars, not as angels battling demons, but as fallen people seeking justice; and we make mistakes. So does every other nation, though our aim is better. Take a further step back, and one sees the whole picture. Without that first sin, none of us would be here. We would have no conflicts, no destructive wants, nothing to divide us. But far from Eden—in the land of pistols *and* ploughshares—we give offense and suffer it, we lose lives and we take them. These things happen because of sin, and it is our fault. Collectively, we are to blame. Yet we can always do the right thing in a fallen world, given the available choices; and sometimes that right thing is war.

Bibliography

Ahern, David O. "Aliens and Citizens: Competing Models of Political Involvement in Contemporary Christian Ethics." In *Faith, Morality, and Civil Society*, edited by Dale McConkey and Peter A. Lawler, 197–208. Lanham, MD: Lexington, 2003.

American Farm Bureau Federation. "Impact of Migrant Labor Restrictions on the Agricultural Sector." February 2006: 1–21. Online: http://www.extension.org/ mediawiki/files/9/91/ labor-econanal06206.pdf.

American Immigration Lawyers Association. "The Border Protection, Antiterrorism, and Illegal Immigration Control Act of 2005 (H.R. 4437), as Amended and Passed by the House on 12/16/05: Section-by-Section Analysis." 9 January 2005. 1–27. Online: http://www.aila. org/content/default.aspx?docid=18258.

Anderson, Leith. "Evangelicals for Immigration Reform." *The Washington Post* (5 April 2009). No pages. Online: http://onfaith.washingtonpost.com/onfaith/panelists/ leith_ anderson/2009/04/evangelicals_for_immigration_reform.html.

Annet, Tim. "Illegal Immigrants and the Economy." *Wall Street Journal* (13 April 2006). No pages. Online: http://online.wsj.com/article/SB114477669441223067.html.

Apgar, Barbara S. and Grant Greenberg. "Using Progestins in Clinical Practice." *American Family Physician* 62 (2000) 1839–46.

Baptist Press. "Hawkins Reports Southern Baptists' Health Statistics are Improving." *Baptist Press*. No pages. Online: http://www.bpnews.net/printerfriendly.asp?ID=23485.

Bratt, James. "The Dutch School." In *Reformed Theology in America: A History of Its Modern Development*, edited by David Wells, 115–34. Grand Rapids, MI: Eerdmans, 1985.

Beavis, Mary Ann. "'Expecting Nothing in Return'" Luke's Picture of the Marginalized." *Int* 48 (1994) 357–68.

Bennett, Brian. "Senators Ask About Cost of Deporting Apprehended Illegal Immigrants." *Tribune Washington Bureau* (29 October 2010). No pages. Online: http://www. azcentral.com/news/articles/2010/10/29/20101029immigration-deportation-gop- senators.html.

Black, Amy E. *Beyond Left and Right: Helping Christians Make Sense of American Politics*. Grand Rapids, MI: Baker, 2008.

Blanchard, Kathryn D. "The Gift of Contraception: Calvin, Barth, and a Lost Protestant Conversation." *JSCE* 27 (2007) 225–49.

Blomberg, Craig. "Give Me neither Poverty nor Riches: A New Testament Theology of Material Possessions." *Stone-Campbell Journal* 2 (1999) 209–26.

Boseley, Sarah. "UN Calls Summit on Spread of 'Lifestyle' Diseases." *The Guardian* (16 September 2011). No pages. Online: http://www.guardian.co.uk/society/2011/sep/16/un-summit-spread-lifestyle-diseases.

Brown, Michael D. *Fair Trade: Reform and Realities in the International Trading System.* London: Zed, 1993.

Burke, Edmund. *Reflections of the Revolution in France,* edited by Thomas H. D. Mahoney. New York: Liberal Arts, 1955.

Carroll R., Daniel. *Christians at the Border: Immigration, the Church, and the Bible.* Grand Rapids, MI: Baker Academic, 2008.

Chaplin, Jonathan. "Conclusion: Christian Political Wisdom." In *God and Government,* edited by Nick Spencer and Jonathan Chaplin, 205–37. London: SPCK, 2009.

Clowney, Edmund P. *How Jesus Transforms the Ten Commandments.* Edited by Rebecca Clowney Jones. Phillipsburg, NJ: P & R, 2007.

Curran, Charles E. "Fertility Control: Ethical Issues." In *Encyclopedia of Bioethics,* edited by W. T. Reich. New York: Simon & Schuster (1995) 2:832–9.

Cutrer, William R. and Sandra L. Glahn. *The Contraception Guidebook: Option, Risks, and Answers for Christian Couples.* Grand Rapids, MI: Zondervan, 2005.

Davis, John Jefferson. *Evangelical Ethics: Issues Facing the Church Today.* 3rd ed. Phillipsburg, NJ: P&R, 2004.

Dell'orto, Giovanna. "Costs Worry Immigration Advocates." *Associated Press* (25 May 2007). No pages. Online: http://www.thehawkeye.com/Story/p0679_BC_Immigration_Lending_ 2ndLd_Writethru_05_24_1129.

Donohue, Brian. "Christie Clarifies: 'Illegal' Immigrants Are in Civil Violation." *Star-Ledger* (29 April 2008). No pages. Online: http://www.nj.com/morristown/index.ssf/2008/04/ christie_clarifies_illegal_imm.html.

Espin, Orlando. "Immigration and Theology: Reflections by an Implicated Theologian." *Perspectivas* (2006) 37–49.

Estes, Daniel J. "Like Arrows in the Hand of a Warrior (Psalm CXXVII)." *VT* 41 (1991) 304–11.

Evangelical Immigration Table. "Evangelical Statement of Principles for Immigration Reform." No pages. Online: http://www.evangelicalimmigrationtable.com.

Gerson, Michael J. "Two Reasons for Civility." *Capital Commentary* (28 January 2011). No pages. Online: http://www.capitalcommentary.org/civility/two-reasons-civility.

Goodnough, Joel. "Redux: Is the Oral Contraceptive Pill an Abortifacient?" *Ethics & Medicine* 17:1 (2001) 37–51.

Gomez, Alan, Jack Gillum, and Kevin Johnson. "U.S. Border Cities Prove Havens from Mexico's Drug Violence." *USA TODAY* (14 July 2011). No pages. Online: http://www.usa today.com/news/washington/2011-07-15-border-violence-main_n.htm.

Grant, Tobin. "SBC Vote Reveals Delicate Evangelical Support for Immigration Reform." *Christianity Today* (29 June 2011). No pages. Online: http://blog.christianitytoday.com/ ctpolitics/2011/06/sbc_vote_reveal.html.

Grisanti, Michael A. "Birth Control and the Christian: Recent Discussion and Basic Suggestions." *The Master's Seminary Journal* 23 (2012) 85–112.

Gramm, Phil. "Reaganomics and the American Character." *Imprimis* 40 (November 2011) 1–3. Online: http://www.hillsdale.edu/news/imprimis/archive/issue.asp?year=2011&month= 11.

Grossman, Cathy Lynn. "Rick Warren Speaks Up on Compassion, Politics, 'Big' Churches." *USA TODAY* (20 September 2009). No pages. Online: http://content.usatoday.com/

communities/Religion/post/2009/09/rick-warren-lords-prayer-compassion-illegal-immigration/1#.UBAX8bRYuSp.

Grudem, Wayne. *Politics According to the Bible*. Grand Rapids, MI: Zondervan, 2010.

Hartford Institute for Religion Research. "Faith Community Today: 2010 National Survey of Congregations: Evangelical Protestant." 1–9. Online: http://faithcommunitiestoday. org/ sites/faithcommunitiestoday.org/files/2010EvangelicalFrequenciesV1.pdf.

Hauerwas, Stanley. *Suffering Presence*. South Bend, IN: University of Notre Dame Press, 1986.

Henry, Paul B.. *Politics for Evangelicals*. Valley Forge, PA: Judson, 1974.

Heschel, Abraham J. *The Sabbath: Its Meaning for Modern Man*. New York: Ferrar, Straus, and Giroux, 1951.

Hinojosa-Ojeda, Raul. "The Economic Benefits of Comprehensive Immigration Reform." *Cato Journal* 32 (2012) 175–99. Online: http://www.cato.org/pubs/journal/cj32n1/cj32n1–12.pdf.

Hippocrates. *The Oath*. Translated by Francis Adam. No pages. Online: http://classics.mit.edu/ Hippocrates/hippooath.html.

Ho, Erica. "Survey: One in Three Americans Would Fail Citizenship Test." *Time* (2 May 2012). No pages. Online: http://newsfeed.time.com/2012/05/02/survey-one-in-three-americans-would-fail-citizenship-test.

Hoefer, Michael, Nancy Rytina, and Bryan Baker. "Estimates of the Unauthorized Immigrant Population Residing in the United States: January 2011." U.S. Department of Homeland Security Office of Immigration Statistics (March 2012) 1–7. Online: http://www. dhs.gov/xlibrary/assets/statistics/publications/ois_ill_pe_2011.pdf.

Hollinger, Dennis. *Individualism and Social Ethics: An Evangelical Syncretism*. Lanham, MD: University Press of America, 1983.

Johnson, Todd. "USA Evangelicals/Evangelicals in Global Context." *Lausanne World Pulse* (January 2006). No pages. Online: http://www.lausanneworldpulse.com/research.php /196/01–2006.

Joyce, Kathryn. *Quiverfull: Inside the Christian Patriarchy Movement*. Boston: Beacon, 2009.

Kasperkevic, Jana. "Deporting All of America's Illegal Immigrants Would Cost a Whopping $285 Billion." *Business Insider* (30 January 2012). No pages. Online: http://articles. businessinsider.com/2012–01-30/news/31004595_1_deportation-kumar-kibble-rob-paral.

Keller, Timothy. *Generous Justice: How God's Grace Makes Us Just*. New York: Dutton, 2010.

King, Martin Luther, Jr. "Letter from a Birmingham Jail." In *I Have a Dream: Letters and Speeches that Changed the World*, edited by James M. Washington, 83–100. New York: Harper Collins, 1992.

Kiyoasaki, Robert. *Rich Dad's Conspiracy of the Rich*. New York: Hachette, 2009.

Lewis, C. S. "The Humanitarian Theory of Punishment." In *God in the Dock: Essays on Theology and Ethics*, edited by Walter Hooper, 287–94. Grand Rapids, MI: Eerdmans, 1970.

Lausanne Committee for World Evangelization. *Scattered to Gather: Embracing the Global Trend of Diaspora*. Manila: LifeChange, 2010.

Longley, Clifford. "Government and the Common Good." In *God and Government*, edited by Nick Spencer and Jonathan Chaplin, 157–79. London: SPCK, 2009.

Lowrey, Annie and Robert Pear. "Doctor Shortage Likely to Worsen with Health Law." *New York Times* (July 28, 2012). Health Section. No pages. Online: http://www.nytimes.com/ 2012/07/29/health/-policy/too-few-doctors-in-many-us-communities.html.

Malchow, Bruce V. "Social Justice in the Israelite Law Codes." *WW* 4 (1984) 299–306.

Marosi, Richard. "Plunge in Border Crossings Leaves Agents Fighting Boredom." *Los Angeles Times* (21 April 2011). No pages. Online: http://articles.latimes.com/2011/ apr/21/local/la-me-border-boredom-20110421.

Marshall, Ellen Ott. *Christians in the Public Square: Faith that Transforms Politics.* Nashville, TN: Abingdon, 2008.

Marshall, Paul. *God and the Constitution: Christianity and American Politics.* Lanham, MD: Rowman and Littlefield, 2002.

Martin, Daniel and James Yankay. "Refugees and Asylees: 2011." U.S. Department of Homeland Security Office of Immigration Statistics (May 2012) 1–7. Online: http:// www.dhs.gov/xlibrary/assets/statistics/publications/ois_rfa_fr_2011.pdf.

Martinez, Juan. "Latin American Theology." Wheaton College Theology Conference 2011: Global Theology in Evangelical Perspective (7 April 2011). No pages. Online: http:// espace.wheaton.edu/media/wetn/BITH/mp3/110407Martinez.mp3.

Matthew, Kenneth A. *Genesis 1–11:26.* NAC 1A. Nashville: Broadman and Holman, 1996.

Meeter, H. Henry. *The Basic Ideas of Calvinism.* Sixth edition. Revised by Paul Marshall. Grand Rapids, MI: Baker, 1990.

Mirkes, Renee. "The Oral Contraceptive Pill and the Principle of Double Effect." *Ethics & Medicine* 18:2 (2002) 11–22.

Miroff, Nick and William Booth. "Arrests of Illegal Immigrants on U.S.-Mexico Border Plummet." *The Washington Post* (3 December 2011). No pages. Online: http://www.washingtonpost.com/world/americas/arrests-of-illegal-migrants-on-us-mexico-border-plummet/2011/12/02/gIQA6Op8PO_story.html.

Mishell, Daniel R., Jr. and Val Davajan. *Reproductive, Endocrinology, Infertility and Contraception.* Philadelphia: F. A. Davis, 1979.

Monger, Randall and James Yankay. "U.S. Legal Permanent Residents: 2011." U.S. Department of Homeland Security Office of Immigration Statistics (April 2012) 1–6. Online: http://www.dhs.gov/xlibrary/assets/statistics/publications/lpr_fr_2011.pdf.

Monsma, Stephen. *Pursuing Justice in a Sinful World.* Grand Rapids, MI: Eerdmans, 1984.

———. "Christian Commitment and Political Life." In *In God We Trust?: Religion and American Politics*, edited by Corwin E. Smidt, 255–69. Grand Rapids, MI: 2001.

Moore, Jeff. "The Fair Trade Movement: Parameters, Issues and Future Research." *Journal of Business Ethics* 53 (2004) 73–86.

Moreland, J. P. "James Rachels and the Active Euthanasia Debate." *JETS* 31 (1988) 81–90.

Mosher, W. D. and J. Jones. *The Use of Contraception in the United States: 1982–2008.* National Center for Health Statistics. *Vital Health Stat* 23/29, 2010.

Mouw, Richard. *He Shines in All That's Fair: Culture and Common Grace.* Grand Rapids, MI: Eerdmans, 2001.

Nathan, Rich. "Hospitality: The Neglected Key to Christian Community." 12 November 2003. 1–17. Online: http://richnathan.org/_media/uploads/files/2003_Sermon_Text/ BuildingACommunityOfHopeInAWorldOfDespair/November8–9.pdf.

National Immigration Forum. "Immigration Enforcement Fiscal Overview: Where Are We, and Where Are We Going?" February 2011. 1–10. Online: http://www.immigrationforum.org/images/uploads/2011/ImmigrationEnforcementOverview.pdf.

NBC News/Wall Street Journal. "Study #12768: NBC News/Wall Street Journal Survey." *MSNBC Media* (July 2012) 1–29. Online: http://msnbcmedia.msn.com/i/MSNBC/Sections/A_Politics/_Today_Stories_Teases/12768_July_Poll.pdf.

Neuhaus, John R. *The Naked Public Square: Religion and Democracy in America.* Grand Rapids, MI: Eerdmans, 1984.

Novak, David. "The Sabbath Day." In *The Ten Commandments for Jews, Christians, and Others,* edited by Roger E. Van Horn, 69–79. Grand Rapids, MI: Eerdmans, 2007.

O'Donovan, Oliver and Joan Lockwood O'Donovan. *From Irenaeus to Grotius.* Grand Rapids, MI: Eerdmans, 1999.

Olson, Dennis T. "Sacred Time: The Sabbath and Christian Worship." In *Touching the Altar: The Old Testament for Christian Worship,* edited by Carol M. Bechtel, 1–32. Grand Rapids, MI: Eerdmans, 2008.

Paral, Rob. "No Way In: U.S. Immigration Policy Leaves Few Options for Mexican Workers." *American Immigration Law Foundation* (July 2005). No Pages. Online: http://robparal. com/downloads/nowayin.htm.

Pasquale, Samuel A. and Jennifer Cadoff. *The Birth Control Book: A Complete Guide to Your Contraceptive Options.* New York: Ballantine, 1996.

Patterson, Richard D. "The Widow, the Orphan, and the Poor in the Old Testament and the Extra-Biblical Literature." *BSac* 130 (1973) 223–34.

Pear, Robert and Carl Hulse. "Immigration Bill Fails to Survive Senate Vote." *New York Times* (28 June 2007). No pages. Online: http://www.nytimes.com/2007/06/28/washington/28 cnd-immig.html.

Pew Hispanic Center. "Modes of Entry for the Unauthorized Migrant Population." Pew Research Center (22 May 2006) 1–5. Online: http://pewhispanic.org/files/factsheets/19.pdf.

Pew Research Center. "Beyond Red vs. Blue: Political Typology." Pew Center for the People and the Press (4 May 2011) 1–155. Online: http://people-press.org/files/legacy-pdf/Beyond-Red-vs-Blue-The-Political-Typology.pdf.

———. "Few Say Religion Shapes Immigration, Environment Views." Pew Center for the People and the Press (17 September 2010). No pages. Online: http://www.people-press.org/2010/09/17/few-say-religion-shapes-immigration-environment-views/.

Piper, John. "What Should We Do About Illegal Immigration?" Desiring God (10 March 2008). No pages. Online: http://www.desiringgod.org/resource-library/ask-pastor-john/what-should-we-do-about-illegal-immigration.

Pohl, Christine. *Making Room: Recovering Hospitality as a Christian Tradition.* Grand Rapids, MI: Eerdmans, 1999.

Polaris Project. "Labor Trafficking in the Restaurant Industry." No pages. Online: http://www. polarisproject.org/human-trafficking/labor-trafficking-in-the-us/restaurants-a-food-service.

Porter, Eduardo. "Illegal Immigrants Are Bolstering Social Security with Billions." *New York Times* (5 April 2005). No pages. Online: http://www.nytimes.com/2005/04/05/business/ 05immigration.html?_r=1.

Pride, Mary. *The Way Home: Beyond Feminism, Back to Reality.* Westchester, IL: Crossway, 1985.

Ramsay, Paul. *Fabricated Man: The Ethics of Genetic Control.* New Haven, CT: Yale University Press, 1977.

Roberts, John. National Federation of Independent Business v. Sebelius 132 S.Ct. 2566, 2593–2594 (U.S., 2012). Online: http://www.supremecourt.gov/opinions/11pdf/11–393c3a2.pdf.

Schrager, Sandra. "Abnormal Uterine Bleeding Associated with Hormonal Contraception." *American Family Physician* 65 (2002) 2073–81.

Schumacher-Matos, Edward. "How Illegal Immigrants Are Helping Social Security." *Washington Post* (3 September 2010). No pages. Online: http://www.washingtonpost.com/wp-dyn/content/article/2010/09/02/AR2010090202673.html.

Shuster, Marguerite. "Response." In *The Ten Commandments for Jews, Christians, and Others*, edited by Roger E. Van Horn, 80–85. Grand Rapids, MI: Eerdmans, 2007.

Singer, Katie. *Honoring Our Cycles: A Natural Family Planning Workbook*. Winona Lake, IN: New Trends, 2006.

Skillen, James. *Christians Organizing for Political Service*. Washington, D.C.: Association for Public Justice Education Fund, 1980.

Smidt, Corwin E. "The Principled Pluralist Perspective." In *Church, State, and Public Justice: Five Views*, edited by Paul C. Kemeny, 127–53. Downers Grove: IL, IVP, 2007.

Snodgrass, Klyne. "Jesus and Money—No Place to Hide and No Easy Answers." *WW* 30 (2010) 135–43.

Soerens, Matthew and Jenny Hwang. *Welcoming the Stranger: Justice, Compassion & Truth in the Immigration Debate*. Downers Grove, IL: InterVarsity Press, 2009.

State of Alabama. "H.B. 56." 25 February 2011. 1–71. Online: http://media.al.com/ht/other /HB56-enr.pdf.

Statue of Liberty-Ellis Island Foundation. "Ellis Island Approaches Centennial of Record-Breaking Day." 29 March 2007. No pages. Online http://www.ellisisland.org/Eiinfo/Press_Centennialrecord.asp.

Storkey, Alan. *A Christian Social Perspective*. Leicester: IVP, 1979.

Sullivan, Dennis M. "The Oral Contraceptive as Abortifacient: An Analysis of the Evidence." *Perspectives on Science and Christian Faith* 58 (September 2006) 189–95.

Tennent, Timothy. "Christian Perspective on Immigration." Asbury Theological Seminary (22 June 2011). No pages. Online: http://www.youtube.com/watch?v=WHx95cuXpUE.

United States Department of State. "Diversity Visa Program, DV 2007–2013: Numbers of Entries Received During Each Online Registration Period by Country of Chargeability." 1–24. Online: http://travel.state.gov/pdf/DV_Applicant_Entrants_by_Country_ 2007-2013.pdf.

———. "Visa Bulletin." August 2012. 1–6. Online: http://travel.state.gov/pdf/visabulletin/visabulletin_August2012.pdf.

United Nations High Commissioner for Refugees. "UNHCR Global Trends 2010: 60 Years and Still Counting." 2011. 1–48. Online: http://www.unhcr.org/4dfa11499.html.

Van Leeuwen, Raymond C. "Be Fruitful and Multiply: Is This a Command or a Blessing?" *Christianity Today* 45:14 (12 November 2001) 58–61.

Wan, Enoch, ed. *Diaspora Missiology: Theory, Methodology, and Practice*. Portland: Institute of Diaspora Studies, 2011.

Wall Street Journal. "America the Uncompetitive." *Wall Street Journal* (August 15, 2008) 814. Online: http://online.wsj.com/article/SB121875570585042551.html?mod=opinion_main_ review_and_outlooks.

Weismiller, David G. "Emergency Contraception." *American Family Physician* (2004) 70 707–14.

Wilks, J., W. F. Colliton, and J. E. Goodnough. "Response to Joel Goodnough, MD, 'Redux: Is the Oral Contraceptive Pill an Abortifacient?" *Ethics & Medicine* 17:2 (2001) 103–15.

Wolsterstorff, Nicholas. *Justice: Rights and Wrongs.* Princeton, NJ: Princeton University Press, 2008.

World Centric. "Fair Trade?" No pages. Online: http://www.worldcentric.org/conscious-living/actionstotake/fairtrade.

Yancey, Philip. *Grace Notes: Daily Readings with a Fellow Pilgrim.* Grand Rapids, MI: Zondervan, 2009.

Young, Brad H. *Jesus the Jewish Theologian.* Peabody, MA: Hendrickson, 1995.

Zernike, Kate. "And Baby Makes How Many?" *The New York Times* (6 February 2009). No pages. Online: http://www.nytimes.com/2009/02/08/fashion/08bigfam.html?pagewanted =all.

Made in the USA
Lexington, KY
11 August 2018